loss *VEGAS*

The Art of Finding Joy in Sin City

Manny Vargas

ISBN: 9798681051930

Library of Congress Control Number: 2016912115

LCCN Imprint Name: Independently published

Dedication

This book is dedicated to my father and my mother. You both mean the world to me, and I am forever grateful for your efforts in raising me. Mom has passed and gone to the heavens, but I know you can read this. I want you to know that I have learned so much from you, and about you, on this journey called life. I just want you both to know how much I love you. And dad, because you are still with me, let's rock 'n' roll throughout the rest of time. After all, I know how much you love the music.

Contents

Author's Note

It is important to point out that the contents of this book are reflective of all my personal experiences: the good, the bad, and the downright ugly. You will see pseudonyms used in some cases to protect the identity of certain individuals. I have regained my passion for learning and, in doing so I decided to learn about myself relentlessly, giving up a life of entertainment to set out for a life of achievement. And with the help of personal development, social and emotional intelligence, family, and friends, I was able to break through. I have used the process in this book to improve my own life and discover joy. My life is always a work in progress but, I know the process works. I owe my deepest appreciation to every person and every resource that has helped me grow. Especially to Coach Rayme, who helped bring out the best in me. I continue to work with her because she's just that good at what she does. She helped me discover the essence of who I am when I was completely baffled and find my voice when I thought she was talking about a physical sound. Without her guidance and support, I might still be trying to fill the shoes of Tony Robbins.

FOREWORD

I've known Manny Patrick Vargas since he was in high school with my daughter, fifteen years ago. At that point, I knew little about him, other than he was a talented baseball player. I love baseball, and after ten years passed, I got word from my daughter he wanted to connect with me and talk about some "business" project he was working on. Because I love to help everyone, I accepted him and some partners of his into my office at the Mandalay Bay, in 2011. I was the Vice President of Retail for Mandalay Bay, Luxor, and Excalibur. Although the project he was pitching was not in my wheelhouse, I connected them with other Presidents and VP's of Food and Beverage in neighboring MGM Resorts properties. And from that point forward, I lost all contact with Manny. Little did I know what was going on in his life!

My life has been a roller coaster of successes and failures. Orphaned at a young age, I moved between many foster homes, and several years later, I ended up at a Missouri Baptist Children's Home. My mother was an addict and drunk, and my father died of cancer. I tell you this to help you understand the connection I have with Manny's life. I always worked hard to make a living, but failed at marriages, until thirty-three years ago, when God blessed me with my current wife, the woman of my dreams. It was at this point I understood what a marriage and family are supposed to be.

Life was good, then the roller coaster started the downhill slide. In 2012, after twenty-three years with MGM Resorts International, my contract was not renewed. I must admit I was a little lost, but our faith kept us moving forward, and then I decided to join my wife in the real estate business. From there, we formed the Tracy Group and are now part of Keller Williams Realty Southwest, running a nice business together.

In 2015, out of the clear blue, Manny found me again, and this time, he wanted to meet for lunch. I was not aware of what he had been through in the years leading to this day, but after several lunches, Manny confided in me about his past: drugs, alcohol, gambling, trouble with love, and failed businesses. This behavior reminded me of what I saw with my mother, growing up in my life. The big difference is that Manny has been blessed with a loving father, aunt, and friends, who have always been in his corner, and because of that, Manny has come out of the fog of drugs, alcohol, and gambling to find new light. It is clear to me, as we continue to spend time together, he has a plan to transform his life, physically and mentally, and he's working that plan everyday.

As he goes on to tell me he's writing a book about life in Las Vegas and how his life was destroyed, then transformed, I suggested he might have missed one important point in his transformation, his relationship with Jesus Christ! But from that point forward, he continued to explore the possibilities he likes to call his spiritual side, and often joins our family for church on Sundays.

I admire what Manny is doing with his life. He has a deliberate plan and works with his own set of coaches, not to mention a family, who is guiding him with love. Manny calls me his spiritual mentor, and even though it might sound strange, this thirty-year-old young man has helped motivate and inspire this sixty-seven-year-old man. I see in him the traits I had as a young man. We often sit around and discuss motivational speakers and authors- Zig Ziglar, Dale Carnegie, Napoleon Hill, Tony Robbins, Og Mandino- we like and what they have added to our lives. Manny has drive, persistence, optimism, and the continual thirst to become a better man. Somewhere along the line, I had lost sight or thought old men can't start over and be great again. I know God brought Manny and I back together, because we needed each other to have an active place in our respective lives. I will enjoy watching Manny's journey through life and am grateful to have an active place in that journey. This book, loss VEGAS-The Art of Finding Joy in Sin City, will provide insight into the dangers and pitfalls of life and what it takes to transform yourself into a healthy, joyful person.

I pray that God will continue to guide and bless Manny and all of you who read this book. Be ready to be *inspired*.

Taryl A. Tracy

INTRODUCTION

For twenty-nine years, eleven months, and six days, I knew, deep down inside my garage of a physical body, that there was a heart and soul. It was a life-form I earned by nature before I was delivered at the Women's Hospital at 2:32 p.m. on January 19, 1986, right here in Las Vegas, Nevada, one mile east of the famed Las Vegas Strip. There was an individualized spirit lurking beneath the surface. Although from my teens to my early and mid-twenties, I didn't quite know what I was capable of, I knew that I had a mountain of potential. But I was fucking clueless on how to tap into it. Or was something else preventing me from reaching inside and pulling back the layers so I could uncover my true self? Why couldn't I overcome the challenges—roadblock after roadblock—on my quest to achieve the life I drew up in my mind? A life full of health, wealth, love, and happiness: Isn't this what everyone wants? I sure did.

Early on, at age ten, I discovered my passion for baseball, and I developed that surprising talent through the collegiate rankings before one last injury crippled me. I had three severe shoulder injuries in the years preceding that one. "I don't think I can afford another one," I said to myself, certainly not at that stage, after a transfer out of the University of San Francisco and a low batting average in my freshman year at the community college. Sure, it was an easy event to blame for the squandering of my college baseball career. I remember that cold, dreary day, perched upon a hilltop in the city of San Bruno at Skyline College, just one mile east of the Pacific Ocean. Our team was going through a series of drills during the afternoon practice when our hulking, angry coach, John, picked up his bat, turned his body in my direction, and then whacked a towering fly ball. I put my head down: "Turn and run!" Thinking about Coach Morrison's voice from my four years in high school, following all of the fundamentals I was taught over the years, I sprinted after a tiny black dot flying through the ocean air with a tailwind on its side. And by the time I pulled my head up to check the speed and distance of the airborne ball, I came crashing into the solid outfield wood fence. My shoulder led the impact and, like a whip, my head came second, blasting the wall. I fell straight to the ground and ended up being taken away in an ambulance.

"You pussy!" I would later think of myself. As it turned out, my right throwing shoulder was separated and, because I have such a big head and a "thick-ass skull," as my dad would always call it, I only ended up with mild wooziness and, surprisingly, no concussion. This injury would sideline me for several months. After my return, I sucked. I couldn't hit an eighty-mile-per-hour fastball coming right into my wheelhouse. Swing and a miss! Strike one! Then two! And three! You're out! "Gosh dammit! Why can't I hit the damn ball anymore?"

"Vargas, sit your ass down, Franky you're in!" Would shout coach.

I failed to work at my craft, and I was giving up on my lifelong dream easily. It was no longer fun for me. The joy I once had playing in little league and the years after was gone, so I decided to quit a few months later.

A teary separation from the game I had been attached to for nine years lurked straight ahead. Did I really suck this bad? Possibly. I know I wasn't working as hard as I should have been. I was more concerned with building up my Myspace friends list and sending private messages to the girls I could find in the Bay Area who fit my standards, from a looks perspective that is. My roommate and I would be sitting on the couch, having lazy computer wars, all the while talking about how we wanted to find our wifeys as teenagers. Hilarious isn't it? Oh, and this was all just before we had all the boys over to shoot the shit and smoke a little weed. "Ah, this is the good life," I would often think to myself. My roommate's parents lived next door and would bring us dinner—yum. We were spoiled, me more so than him because it was his house, but I didn't even have to pay rent. It wasn't the right time for me to be selfish, but somehow I always was. Maybe it was because I was an only child, and I was just doing what I knew.

After leaving my heart in San Francisco, I quickly realized the real world was here. No more daddy's money, no more living rent free, no more running around San Francisco free of worry. What the hell was I going to do now? I was terrified. As both a child and a teen, my one and only goal was to play baseball. I was good enough to play in the majors. I know that, but I pissed away all of my opportunity because I preferred to simply be lazy. If you had asked me what I wanted to do growing up, I would have told you I *will* be a professional baseball player. It was the dream I nurtured in my mind.

Soon after my return home, I was hired for my first restaurant job on the Las Vegas strip. I am home, baby! Let's make some noise—this is my city! I made great money for a nineteen-year-old kid. I mean, I was making four grand a month, with no responsibility just yet. It was during my short tenure at this job that I was introduced to the sultry temptation of gambling. Some of my coworkers would invite me out to the local bars after work. "But I am not of age," I would say. "No worries, man, I know the bartender." Of course, I opted in. I was trying to people-please, and I made sure that I wouldn't create any enemies at the workplace. I needed some allies, so I found a way to into the mix, something I seemed to learn through the years. How? I don't know. I think it was more of an innate gift.

Most nights ended with us sitting at Brewsky's from midnight until sunrise, hanging out with my man Dano. I am still not sure if he knew I was underage, but he didn't give a shit because I was putting my hard-earned money right into the bar machines. I had to polish hundreds of racks of wine and water glasses and clear a lot of dirty plates to make that money. I am surprised I don't have arthritis as a result. I killed it (made a lot of money) most nights, so naturally I believed it was playtime. Ah, but who cares if I'm getting used to blowing money away. "I don't have any bills, so let's get a thrill, all the while sipping ice cold Bud Lights, dropping the Baileys Irish Cream with whiskey into the Guinness, which results in Irish Car Bombs, for those of you who are unaware. In any case, I definitely got bombed. It wasn't unusual for me to stumble out to my car—often the wrong car—and scratch the hell out of my door handle, or theirs, because I was too drunk to see and just "get it in the hole." How did I drive home? God only knows. After waking up with a pulsing headache and a mouth dryer than the Mojave Desert, I would panic, "oh shit! Where's my phone?" This would happen as I scrambled in the bed, throwing sheets in all directions. I never moved so fast in my life. I would then get up and sprint around the house, examining the damage. Usually there were some left over ninety-nine-cent tacos from Jack in the Box and a bottle of booze somewhere nearby. "But where is my phone? Maybe it fell in between the cracks of the bed. Let me go look." I would throw the mattress into the air and it was like I struck gold. "Oh look! There it is. How did it get down on this side where my feet rest at night? Oh man…I have no idea." But for now, I still have my *life* in my fingertips.

Eight months later, I had the brilliant idea of running away to Los Angeles. Several months before, during a vacation, some Russian woman on Miami Beach asked me, "Are you a model?"

Say what? Yes. I am not kidding; she really said that. So what did I do? I believed it! Shit, I am a good-looking mofo. Let me take my talents to Venice Beach and give this runway lifestyle a chance. One day, I was so excited, because I was on my way to meet an agent, driving down Ventura Boulevard heading west into Sherman Oaks. Here I was thinking, "Oh man, this was the right choice! I've got this. I mean, look at this Chia Pet hairdo, my nice sparkly smile, my brown skin—they are going to love me." Ha! Man, was that a bunch of nonsense or what? They told me I needed to get headshots from "this guy" down the street whom they work with and, because I was naïve, I said, "Really, you want me to get headshots? Let's do it!"

"It's going to cost a gazillion dollars," the guy said.

"Sure." I have no money, but fuck it, I'm in, whatever I have.

"Call us when you get them done, kid."

You bet I was scammed. I never heard from them again, so I became a menace to Hollywood, not South Central.

I moved into a bachelor unit in West Hollywood where the shower, bathroom, and closet all shared my sleeping space. As if being claustrophobic wasn't already causing me to press the panic button, this place made me feel like I was being taken in behind bars for no reason. It was so bad that, during one evening when they stayed with me, my best friend could be heard banging his girlfriend two feet away in the shower. "Do I really want to hear this right now?" Come on guys, keep it down. I am not sure if the moaning is getting me excited or pissing me off, because I'm half asleep and I am definitely not getting up to walk out. Where were my headphones when I needed them?

I was such a cool LA cat. I moved around Los Angeles three different times and even slept on my cousin's hardwood floor in her studio apartment with not only her, but her boyfriend as well. *I slept on the hardwood floor,* and that was painful on my back, no kidding. I had no friends, even though I tried desperately to make them. I would do anything, but nothing worked and no person wanted anything to do with me as long as I wasn't one of the cool guys, driving a Mercedes Benz, with a nice house in the hills, or rolling into the club buying $400 bottles of vodka. So what did I do? I bought in!

I drove my ass home to Las Vegas. After looking online at new cars, I spotted the coolest car I could afford at the time and called dad to ask if he would help me. "Not this time, boy!" I made the purchase for the sole reason of fitting in. Why not, right? I thought I was the model celebrity, driving his car around the streets of Hollywood, up and down Santa Monica Boulevard, and over into the Hollywood Hills to see if I couldn't attract a few pairs of eyes. The funny part was...it was a Dodge Charger. Not just an ordinary Dodge Charger, but one that had twenty-two-inch rims for style and Lamborghini doors for sizzle. I would roll up to the club and, of course, I would always park valet. Shit, I'd get out and make sure the doors went up. That's right, I've arrived, I'd tell myself, but in reality I was broke and it was all a facade. I was such a bonehead, and I was extending my financial means because I figured I had to be like the other rich folks of Beverly Hills.

There was one bright spot in LA. It was her hair and her eyes, a gorgeous, blond, maturing woman, who was twenty-six when I met her at the Beverly Hills Hotel. A tall, smoking hot Cajun girl from just south of New Orleans, she had blue cat eyes that I'm sure made all of the housewives of Beverly Hills jealous. My first thought was, "Man, I would love to sleep with that woman, but she's out of my league," and she should be starring next to Jay Baruchel as the female lead.

But hold on. Maybe I could? So just be your arrogant, aggressive young self, I told myself, and go for it. Everyone was after her; she was pretty as they come and, after a casual night out with coworkers, we got close— like real close, smooching and flirting and "Whoa, is this really happening?" We started dating, and it didn't take long to learn about her history, friends, boyfriends, and family, and that I was nowhere near the level of the men she dated. In fact, right before I met her, she went on some dates with a famous casino owner from right here in Las Vegas and a well-known owner of an NFL team. How could I match up? I felt obligated to prove myself. The pressure was mounting, and I began to make foolish financial decisions. Don't forget, I was twenty-one, so making decisions that would get me in a rut were not thought through, ever! I was such a putz, and I was doing things that were way beyond me. I figured I had to be like the other millionaires around the block to please this goddess. I'd take us out for dinner almost every night— El Compadre on Sunset Boulevard was a tasty destination, but expensive. Bars were around the corner on Hollywood Boulevard, next to Grauman's Chinese Theatre and the Kodak facility, and she was quite used to being taken out, wined, dined, jetted, and limoed all over the place. "Hmm, but be careful Manny, I think I'm starting to act a little bit like this one," said my subconscious. I just wanted someone to spend time with, and I would have done just about anything to make sure I was holding her attention. And if going broke was the solution, then I had the formula; literally scraping pennies together in an effort to afford the pleasure of hitting Six Flags, Universal Studios, or the Grove for a movie night. By the time Hollywood chewed me up and spit me out, I was starting to reconsider why I was still there.

It was a quick nine months in LA. "Daddy, I'm coming home again," but this time with some extra baggage: my lovely blond girlfriend. Holy shitballs, what was I thinking? Well, clearly I wasn't, but let me just tell the truth and get this off my chest. It's time. It didn't go well, and many years later, all the way up until she found out I was writing this book, I learned I still had some pain to heal.

"Congrats on your book. I hope you did not mention my name in there, though," she said in a text message I knew was coming.

"Thank you. Your name is not used," I replied with a smiley face to end the response.

Another message: "Did you mention something about me or us? Or change my name?"

"You are not mentioned, nor is your name used, but it's a story of my life, and you were around in some of my troubled times."

"Yeah, no shit! So did you use a different name? And that is your perspective of events, not necessarily the truth. And I'm sure you left out some very important details. I think it would be wise if you show me that part."

That led to a phone call, then yelling, then blaming, then arguing—all of which disturbed my inner peace. I was bothered for several days, and this woman was able to successfully mess up my inner workings and take me back to a nasty place that I had lived through already. How could this happen? I had worked so hard for the last eight months to get to this point. I'll be honest; the first thing I wanted to do was come back to this paragraph and write a bunch of messed-up shit about her because she pissed me off. She pushed my buttons, and as if I were in a time machine, I went back to the old me.

In fact, originally, I did write some negative words, things like "bitch," "sorry ass," and "grow up," but who would that have made me? How would I get better from that? So I hit backspace on a whole paragraph and chose not leave it here, because what she said is the truth, and I need to let the world know that in order to get better, you have to accept your fuckups, no matter how troubling they may be. I had to go back to basics and do more deep inside work to solve this problem.

This can show you how deeply the editing of a book can go. I am days away from finalizing the editing, and here I am making a change because I noticed a repair was necessary. It's the right thing to do.

So here are the very important details I was ashamed to mention. Yes, I threw her out of my dad's at twenty-one because I was an asshole. Yes, she moved away from her agency to live in Las Vegas, and sure, I sold her on the idea. Yes, she called the cops on me after I shoved her to the ground. Yes, I destroyed some of her most prized possessions in the street because I was emotionally unavailable, and last, the haymaker—yes, I gave her a common STD at the time we dated.

She has a right to be angry with me forever, right? Yes, she does. I had to learn that I can't make amends to everyone, nor be everyone's friend. The scarring is done, and as a result I can now see where the frustration comes from. She thinks I'm a piece of shit, and she doesn't have to be happy for me. I got so used to blaming her that I forgot to look in the mirror. Fine, I accept that. The fact that I was twenty-one makes no difference; the fact that I was immature makes no difference. It was my time to man up, at thirty, for the shit that I put her through, and doing so doesn't negate the fact that it happened and that she is still hurt by it.

I was trying to prove my victory in life at this point— no, that's not what you should do, Manny. Now I am assuming responsibility for the effects I've had on her. I did not objectively take control of this built-up resentment. I just boxed it up and put it in the closet. These were my behaviors, and I wanted her to see I had grown up, that I was better, but the reality is I just needed to do something else—maybe say thanks, or sorry. That simple. I can't blow it off anymore and make an excuse because we've been out of the relationship for a long time.

I assume responsibility for the way you feel. I misused my resentment. If you are reading this, I just want to say, I'm sorry, and thank you for helping me on this journey and being part of my developing story. I learned things about me that I wouldn't have known otherwise. Thank you for the information. I move forward now knowing what I don't like and what I do like in my life, which are both equally important. On we go...

In the meantime, I was itching to try something new because life was pulling me harshly. I was trying a lot and moving from restaurant job to restaurant job, but I had no clue where I was headed because I couldn't keep still. I liked the on-the-go approach, and here I was just going with the flow. I think I was trying to narrow my focus on life. I was accepted at Florida International University to further my studies and possibly make a move to be nearer to the only other family I had outside of Vegas; but because of fear, and not having the resources to make such a huge cross-country move, I enrolled back into school locally. After a stellar spring and summer term at the community college, though, I dropped out because I wanted something else. Was I crazy? Who knows? But it was a nice to know that my brain still worked.

Age twenty-two came and went like a snapchat, twenty-three like the blink of an eye, and then at twenty-four, my eyes were wide open. I had had enough of handling dirty plates of food and people yelling at me for a new fork because they just dropped one on the floor. I was ready for a change and eager to surround myself with more excitement: high energy, hot chicks, pulsing sound systems, neon lights, going out…After all, I was already partying like a rock star. In high school, I was throwing my own gigantic parties. In San Francisco, the same thing; in LA, I tore up the boutique clubs and lounges after I found my coolness. Just maybe, I thought, this was a good indicator for the proper direction of my life. World-class entertainment, including the best musicians and DJs on the planet, were on their way into Las Vegas.

"Yo, Vargas, I am applying to this new place that is being built at the Encore. They say it is supposed to transform the nightlife scene out here!" No way, Tryst and Tao are the bomb! How could anything beat Tryst, with its upscale, classy, and lavish style and decor that makes up that electrifying venue? Have you seen that ninety-foot waterfall that stands as a center focal point when you walk in? And the mini-lake next to the dancefloor? It's romantic, with sexy red lining up the whole club. Man, I pulled all kinds of chicks there. Remember that one time we were getting hyphy on the dance floor to E-40's 'Tell Me When To Go'—you are the goofiest white boy I know…!"

"Dude, that was all the time."

"Dancing with sweat dripping down our foreheads, and all the girls wanted us!"

"Bro, I applied, and you should think about it. It's the same guys that run Tryst that are building XS! And with a name like that, maybe it will outdo what we know as the 'best.' I hear these nightclub staff make a killing," said my friend.

"All right, I'll look into it."

I applied the same day. I was very fortunate, as I got through six rounds of interviews, beating out thousands of candidates all competing for the same position, and I didn't even have an advantage like many of my future coworkers did by "knowing" someone in management or in the business already. Shit, I hit the lotto. I died and went to heaven, and I was now being paid to live, breathe, and earn money in this environment. XS was no average club, either. It is arguably the world's best nightclub, still, today.

During my time working in the nightclub, I was also pursuing outside business opportunities. My reason for dropping out of college was to pursue my new desire, or dream, of owning my own business. If I took the nightclub job, which clearly I did, I would have more flexibility to travel, more flexibility in my schedule, and an unlimited ability to network. So I thought, let's keep it real, Manny, you just wanted to party your ass off! I had this idea that wealthy people should be my friends and, with my personality, I was out to build relationships with them in order to have them *give* me some money for upcoming projects. The Wynn-Encore properties were the epicenter of affluent folks spending hundreds of thousands of dollars nightly inside the club. And for what?

An oversized bottle of champagne, vodka, or tequila…or hundreds of such bottles in this case; the pleasure of having twenty-five paid girls there, escorts, or hookers if you will, who take their pants off at the drop of a dime; or maybe it was because the big spender would get his or her name up on the LED screen just for spending $50,000 on a wooden table that may have cost $100 to manufacture, and spending another fortune for a $12 bottle of champagne marked up 1 million percent. Ha! And don't forget the round sticker, with a picture of a person smiling while holding up two $10,000 bottles of champagne. Did you wake up the next day feeling good, dude? Aren't there other economic uncertainties where that money could be made more useful? I'd say a few people are your good friends, if that, but that the other 99 percent of the group was freeloading. Did you get the number of the girl from New York who has daddy issues and just likes to use men for money? Or how about the other forty people who are just drinking your alcohol, but you have no idea who they are? I know, because I would get the answers straight from all the drunken folks right there in front of me. However, this was the reality and this is Vegas. I was definitely jealous. If they didn't care, then neither did I.

I constantly put myself in a position to embarrass and humiliate my livelihood by striking a conversation with customers, on purpose, and mostly with men, many times exchanging phone numbers or contact information in the hope of a follow-up e-mail or call to pitch my business ideas to them. "How come you are always talking to so many guys and asking for their phone numbers?" The staff would ask and always laugh at me for my efforts. "Are you gay?"

"Oh stop, you don't get it." I would brush it off. I have hundreds of napkins from those nights with names and phone numbers on them, including owners of multimillion-dollar businesses, artists, and athletes. At one time, I was text messaging with football star Jerome Bettis, nicknamed "The Bus," just to name one. There were many others. I would approach them at table 500, table 320, and table 705, near the stripper pole, where I once took care of Beyoncé after her concert there. Yes, Beyoncé. I was responsible for servicing these tables on any given night, so why not mingle with the who's who of the world. It was part of the job, or at least I made it that way. I had no shame, and I ended up having several meetings and built several relationships.

I was so active in my pursuit that, one day, it ended up biting me in my ass. One of the customers I talked with was a friend of the manager. Oops! Oh well, I was trying. I'll never forget the day I was called into the office and disciplined by management. One of my managers said to me, "Nobody cares about your stupid yogurt shop." This happened to be the project I was pitching and, to be honest, I was thinking, "Fuck you, you have no clue what I am up to, you piece of shit!" Clearly, I was ready to rip his head right from his shoulders. Anyway, I was damn close to getting a few deals done, but simultaneously nervous because I very well could have lost my job, forcing me back into the open market and into something I probably would not have enjoyed as much. So I settled for the suspension that they gave me.

I ended up leaving my nightclub job several years later because my dreams did come true. I am a restaurant owner! Yes! I was able to raise outside funds from a group of investors and buy two casual, fast-food chicken restaurants. Soon after, I opened up a third storefront. This was an entirely different concept—For Goodness Shake—a create-your-own milkshake shop with dazzling candies, flavorful cookies and cereals, and tasty fruits. For each milkshake we sold, we bought a meal for a hungry child in need. The discouraging truth is that I thought all the work was done after we got over the hump of opening.

Oh, the opening—let me tell you about that. Friends and Family Day was on Monday, June 24, 2013, and I was "gone" for three straight days, raving my ass until the early morning at the promise land of Electric Daisy Carnival (EDC), a giant festival with carnival elements and the world's best lineup of DJs playing for one hundred thousand jumping music fans. It was nearing four o'clock in the morning, Monday, and I remember thinking to myself: "Oh man, we only have one more DJ left, and this afternoon I have to be at the store for the kickoff. But, first, let me take a selfie! And pop one more molly!" That should keep me alive for the next several hours, I thought. I had prepped my staff and partners on my absence, but told them I would be just fine come opening time. "Dude, you want to be a successful businessman, but you are out partying the day of your opening? You have a lot to learn son, you'll get yours…" That was God's voice there. Running restaurants was nowhere near as fun as I had originally thought. The thrill was gone once I realized the workload and, honestly, I was deficient in the knowledge to know what I was up against and how much effort it would take. Effort being the key word, and something I had failed to learn over the years. I thought the world would be mine, the people and systems would just fall into place, wishing and hoping everything would work out.

Six months after opening the shake shop, after all the buzz, the press, write-ups in the magazines and newspapers, and feeling like I was making progress, I found that our business was about ready to shut down because we weren't generating enough revenue.

"Stephanie, how did we do today? Were our numbers good? Were there a lot of people through the doors?"

"Yeah, it was good!"

"Ah, you're always so positive! What were the numbers?"

"Well, we did six hundred and thirty dollars in gross sales."

"Ouch!"

I should have let her run the place; she probably would have done a much better job than me. My staff was great, seasoned employees whom I stole from other great companies like Starbucks and The Coffee Bean & Tea Leaf. They were always willing to learn and had great faith in our potential, but their distracted leader was the one bad link. I was beginning to think, "We're not going to make it." Our six months of free rent was up, payroll was high, and with no surprise, I closed its doors in November 2013. And fuck me sideways, but the other two, I found out, were sending distress signals, too. All three of my restaurants were about to implode. I painfully failed at finding a solution. My partners were as distraught as the staffs. I was just as emotional and fearful of what was going to happen next, but the problems were only beginning. My new babies were robbed by my own lack of resourcefulness. I lost a lot of people's money, and now I was the hated one. I didn't like this feeling, but they didn't care. They trusted me, and I let them down…

I knew lawsuits were on their way, and I didn't have the money to pay on any of those. I barely had enough to pay my bills and bankruptcy followed. To make matters worse, the one woman who I loved dearly and who put up with so much of my bullshit was leaving me because I had abused my privilege to be loved and cared for. "Her Name Is…and She Dances on the Sand." We met on the late night/early morning of January 4 of the fresh year of 2012, which originally started out as the first industry night for a new nightclub in the Bellagio Hotel. Hyde is the name, and industry night is a dedicated evening where the nightclub invites the locals who work in restaurants, bars, clubs, or anywhere, really, in Las Vegas a place to party like the tourists do. Hyde, an intimate setting centered with an open view of the popular fountains, gives partygoers excellent visuals of towering sprouts of water with thousands of onlookers oohing and aweing. Bally's, Paris, and Planet Hollywood sit loftily in the backdrop. I was there, chillin' with a couple buddies of mine, jammin' to the beat of the music the DJ was spinnin'. Most of us were hanging around in the same vicinity because our staff had an adjacent main floor table to support the venue. I used to tell Romance that I would tell this story when we would get married, during a toast, because it's quite funny and an unusual way to meet a lady for the first time. It worked and led me to some great memories, but clearly no marriage. I was sitting on top of a box next to the table, trying to be invincible, because, I mused, "If this security guard asks me one more time to get down, I am going to punch him in the goddamn face." But I'm calm…and rollin' hard, teeth fucking grinding, and I'm sucking on the inside of my cheeks with an occasional eye drift into the back of my head. It was not a good time to speak with anyone, but when a mutual friend of ours came up to me and started a conversation, I participated. They were both dancers at XS, so it was very strange that I hadn't officially met Romance yet. But this night there would be no excuse. She was dancing a step away from the two of us, talking about I have no gosh-damn idea, but she turned for a second, talked to her cut-loose friend, and picked up something funny, and it wasn't until I was relayed the message that I got the reason for her chuckle. "She looked at me and obviously felt it was OK to tell me that she was just told, "She wants somebody to bend her over and dah…dah…dah…dah…dah (you think of that one). "What?" I mean, I was high, but are you serious? I wasn't sure if I was being asked to help solve a problem, or if I really heard this. I guess this was my lucky night. So I wasted no time in starting a conversation, which lasted thirty minutes, then an hour, and then a few hours in, when we were clearly getting somewhere. After a few hours in, though, I wasn't interested in just trying to blow my load with this one; she was different. I had been single for some time, in and out of dating, and I never got serious because of how picky I was. This woman was intelligent and radiating love, a natural from the Midwest. I asked questions. Why are you here? How long have you been here? And with every answer, I got sucked in just a little bit more

"I am ready to go home," she said.

"Would you like me to take you? I have my big ugly friend with me (who I was also driving home), but I don't mind dropping you off."

I guess our mutual friend vouched for me, because she didn't hesitate in leaving with me. We walked to the car, holding hands. I was lit up! I get so excited holding hands, and I felt a severe connection with her. "I forgot my keys," I said as we got to the car, so I had to run back into the club and grab them from a friend who was holding them for me before sprinting back through the casino. My juices were flowing, and I was in a loving mood, for many reasons. As I passed the front desk, a lady fixing the flower garden with hundreds of roses was just sitting there. Ah, this is perfect!

"Ma'am, do you mind if I take one of these?"

"No. I am sorry, you cannot," she replied.

I could barely understand her, but we were the same brown color. "I've got this," I thought to myself. "I just met a very awesome lady, and I want to delicately surprise her when I get back to the car here in a few seconds," I explained, using hand gestures to aid in my begging. The smile and upward motion of her cheeks told me she understood.

"Take it."

"You're the best, thank you," and off I went. "Here, I got this for you." I smiled, and I handed her the rose from behind my back where I was hiding it. I was hopeful that I maintained myself well enough on drugs so she would decide to see me again. She never knew I was high when we met because I was afraid to tell her for all of those years. Anyway, we ended up dating for several years, but now I am stuck trying to clean up a mess. Dear lord, my world was coming to an end, and I was all over the place.

After being hired for a low-income- job as a food and beverage manager at McCarran International Airport, a place I disliked and was miserable because it was a dump, I felt I had to start over somewhere. This place served no benefit for me (aside from being able to get on a plane); I was freshly out of my business and out of a life. At the same time, I found the courage to battle for the love of Romance, who had left my sorry ass. The months were passing and I was torn. She wanted nothing to do with me at the beginning, but I was stoic in my pursuit to show her it was meant to be. I fought tooth and nail. I would show up with candies from the Starbucks and leave them on her doorstep, I would use my friends as bait to get her near me so I could confess, and, on one evening, I even found out her coordinates. I needed to tell her how I felt! It was scary, but I had no other choice. She wouldn't respond to me, I couldn't be alone, and yet I was so reliant on her. She was that great, and did I really fuck this up? How many times are you going to ruin things, Manny? Believe it or not, after a relentless pursuit that came from my heart, I ended up, for the time being, proving to Romance how much I cared for her and how badly I couldn't be without her. I was dependent and the joke was on me. After being fired from my food and beverage manager position, I filed for unemployment. I started to sell drugs to earn money because I had none. I had a problem spending money and couldn't stash any away if my life depended on it. Maybe, just maybe, it was because I was still thinking like I was back during my time in LA? So what could be worse? Well, here you go. I had been moving drugs around for a long time, aiding visitors in getting the goods. So I came up with a story that, "I wasn't a drug dealer—I was just helping people out." Bullshit, Manny, you are a drug dealer, and this was my next source of income.

Well, guess what? Just when I thought things were clearing up in my relationship, I sabotaged it, for the last and final time. I knew it was coming, and there was no chance of selling myself back into this one. I already saved my ass one too many times, and I used every story I could to preserve the fiddling companionship. What was wrong with me and women? Why was I so jealous and envious of love? I wanted to be in control of her life and keep her as close to me as possible, so that I could avoid that fear of being all by myself one more time; a fear I couldn't escape.

This breakup fucked me up, and I went into another downward spiral. I did anything I could to make myself feel better. Booze, coke (not cola), and "raging" all topped the list; I was going nuts! I was out every night, doing anything to make the pain go away. I used this as a method to cover up the damage when, in all reality, I was so torn up inside nothing in life mattered. I started to make up stories in life that made me feel better. I was on a rampage, behaving against my morals, which gave me temporary satisfaction. I felt myself going backward in life, and I was only twenty-seven. Job after job rolled by—territory sales rep for Eat 24, which I quit, marketing specialist for a local digital marketing company, where I was fired, account manager for Berkeley Communications, nope, didn't do it, and, finally, a silly position on the Strip, asking people to watch NBC-TV shows to make a buck, which I made sure would work. Then, I was on the brink of launching another business when that all fell apart and crushed another important friendship. Hosting and promotions? "Ah, I love this, but that's nightlife, and I don't want to go backward." Well, maybe sometimes you need to clean up other areas of your life to be really good at something and to find out who you really are, is what I would learn down the road. Everything was going wrong because I was going about everything wrong. I was not being honest with myself in my pursuit of a fulfilled life, and I certainly was not equipped with the life skills, tools, and resources to battle any of the difficult times.

Is Life Really This Tough?

Join me on the remainder of this ride as I lose control, regain it again, swerve, and then arrive safely at my destination. I made a choice to choose joy and, in my decision-making, I found life got really awesome. No really, I am being serious...*enjoy*!

PART ONE:
THE STRUGGLE

Chapter 1
What Happens in Vegas...I Do All the Time

"The truth will set you free, but first it will piss you off."

—*Gloria Steinem*

Las Vegas, Nevada, early Friday morning, November 6, 2015. The 9:00 a.m. sun was anxious to get my ass out of bed, creeping through the smallest crack in the closed blinds. "But it's too early, can't I sleep in a little bit more? I feel like I just went to bed!" The other foggy reality I was having amounted to, "Oh gosh, I am still hammered." I woke up and there was no doubt I was still drunk from the night before. It was time for recall—I just came off a blowout night, on and off the Las Vegas Strip.

"Manny! What are you drinking? This one is on me!" said Ryan.

"Vodka soda with a lime, please."

"You got it."

Two vodka sodas, something else I don't remember, and some fireball shots were ordered from the bartender. "Here you are," she says and hands over the bill.

"Zazdarovje!" he shouted as we all put our arms up in the air to celebrate an early round of shots.

"This is going to be a fun night. Are you guys excited?" I asked. The evening was off to a great start at the Hard Rock Hotel. I was invited to watch my friend's fourteen-year-old son, Trel, play his first big electronic dance music show for another group of friends' company, Ravealation, so I invited friends I thought would be interested in coming down to support him. The group included my newest lady friend, Amor.

"Guys, is everyone ready for another round?" They asked.

"Yes! Let's do it!" I responded.

I was on a mission to get drunk and be the life of the party, which I was known for in embarrassing fashion. We were already turning up, and it wasn't even show time! The show started at 9:00 p.m., and our DJ friend was the first act on, playing for thirty minutes. I had already figured out my next move, after his set, because I had to keep the evening going at a good pace. "But slow down sunshine, you have some friends here, hang out with them, don't just drink and dash…you can spend a few hours here. Let's catch some more of the show." This was an inner conversation. "All right, then, let's keep drinking!" And that's what we did, exchanging bill after bill, dancing foolishly, and sharing some good quality time together until it was time for me to make my way over to the next party, pretty much wasted at this point. Thanks everyone.

"You're leaving, dude?"

"Yeah, thanks for coming, guys. I appreciate it. It's been real."

"Great to see you, Manny."

This would be the last time I see a few of these guys for a long time!

I had other close friends visiting from Ohio. I met these gentlemen earlier in the summer, at a pool party and, because they were so kind and welcoming, we ended up spending a majority of a Sunday and Monday together. Friends of mine and I were invited up to their tower suite at the Encore Hotel, after the daytime pool fun, to get loose and engage in pregame festivities before making our way down to the Sunday night-swim party at XS. I had been back at XS many times before just tonight. Many times. How could I discard my vice? I would not. We did have an unforgettable time that early summer weekend and, because these guys were the real deal, we made it a point to stay in touch. On this trip, they were celebrating a birthday and, on this night, the party was at one of the older, but still poppin', nightclubs, TAO, inside the Venetian Hotel. I couldn't wait to get over there and turn up. When I arrived at the nightclub, they were seated on the main dance floor, with a center-stage table facing the performers' wall. Gigantic bottles of champagne, patron, vodka—you name it—were there. Juicy J was the entertainer for the night, Three 6 Mafia! And, in traditional fashion, when it was his time to come on and rap, he "murdered it."

"I gotta stay fly iiiiiiii, until I die iiiiii

I gotta stay fly iiiiiiiii, until I die iiiiii

I gotta stay flyiiiiiiiiiiii, until I die iiiiii

I gotta stay fly iiiiii, until I die iiiiii

Call me the juice and you know I'm a stunt

Ride in the car with some bump in the trunk

Tone in my lap and you know it's the pump

Breakin' down the good weed rollin' the blunt

Ghetto pimp tight girls say I'm the man

Ice on the wrist with the ice in the chains"

He had everyone bouncing, singing, from side to side on their legs, arms moving in sync with their lower halves, as he had a bottle in one hand rocking the same motions during his performance. His flow was tight and the crowd loved him, our table included. Just about the same time he started his performance, I was handed some ecstasy pills.

"Manny! Here. Take these. I am leaving tomorrow, I have too many, plus this weekend has been rough!"

"What the hell are these? They are green. I have never seen green press pills."

"They are pressed molly."

"What the fuck, I didn't even know they made these, and I have done a great deal of drugs in the last several years! But, here, give them to me! Gulp."

This would mean my night was going to fade quickly out, and I would be out cold for the evening. I had a bad habit of blacking out when drinking vodka, tequila, and champagne topped off with drugs (especially if I didn't have any cocaine or Adderall to keep me going). What a tasty combination. Not. But I loved to do it, and I abused the toxic combination all the time. "Ah, who gives a rat's ass, I play just as hard as everyone else." But don't you live here in Vegas, Manny? So. That didn't stop me and, quite frankly, it didn't matter that I do.

The problem with my blackouts amounts to more than just making a complete fool out of myself, like this one time.

"Guys you have no idea what I did last night," I would fess up to my friends the next day.

"What, man?"

"I threw up in my car while I was driving home on the two fifteen freeway to get back home!"

"No way, that's gross! How do you know?"

"I can't remember, but when I got into my car after basically sleeping all day, I was greeted by the residual vomit not just lining the inside of the door panel, but on the outside too!"

"Ah, come on man, yuck."

"Yeah, clearly I was trying to stick my head out of the window and, the trippy part is, I had a blast!"

"You have a problem, Manny. Who does that?"

Or another time, risking my life one July Fourth holiday, racing my car down a local road in excess of eighty miles per hour against my buddy.

"You want to race, pussy?"

"I'll smoke you!"

Engines build up the rpms and we're off! We thought we were on a NASCAR track in a forty-mile-per-hour speed zone. That could have ended in me killing someone or myself. Believe it or not, we raced the length of the drive home, a good ten miles. And, almost always, a woman has been on the receiving end of my inconsistent, grotesque behavior, and on this particular night, it was no different. As I woke up in the morning from that bothering sun, feeling fucking angry for feeling like shit, and after asking myself, "Oh my God, what happened?" I looked over the edge of my bed and, on the right side, I saw laying a packed suitcase, positioned like it was ready to grow legs and walk out of my place and onto a plane. On my left, as I rolled over to take a look, I was relieved to see Amor.

My heart dropped because I had been here before. Immediately, I felt like I had fucked up, and the internal conversation began.

"Uh oh, I blacked out. What did I do to her? Please, God, tell me I didn't fight with this woman last night at some point. I don't remember the second half of the night. Wooooow," I would say aloud, as if this would lighten the mood. She wasn't having any part of it! "Shit, I fucked up. I hope the damage is minor, because I like this girl." She was sitting upright in my bed with the most pissed off look on her face and, if I could have read her mind, I'm sure it would have said, "Who is this monster?" When I decided to ask more and figure out the final details of the night, she replied with some repulsive words and facial expressions. I asked, "OK. What happened?" and the first thing she said to me was, "*I don't even know who you are anymore*."

"Well, I am Manny. Shut up your cocky-fuck face, this girl is about to tell you how shitty you are."

"I wanted to leave the hotel and come home, but you wanted to stay! You practically fought me all the way out of the casino and into the cab! You even threatened to leave me by myself in a city that I had just come across the world to see you in!"

Amor just flew across the globe to visit and spend a week in the United States with me. I started to have immense fear and flashbacks through all of my previous years where I went through the same disgusting experiences as a result of my behavior after drinking. It was like a flipbook through time, from 2004 to November 6, 2015. I didn't want to lose yet another woman after another of the same mistakes. *I. Have. Heard. Those. Words. One. Too. Many. Times.* And had those empty stomach feelings, like my insides have just been ripped out, one too many times, and it was just getting too hard to deal with. I knew I wanted better. I had all of the right intentions, but something was in the way, and I couldn't control my desire to party if my life depended on it.

Amor and I had met two months prior, right here in my backyard and, when I say my backyard, I mean a town called Paradise; yes, this was my home. Paradise is a town adjacent to the city of Las Vegas. The town of Paradise contains McCarran International Airport; the University of Nevada, Las Vegas; and most of the Las Vegas Strip. Paradise contains most tourist attractions in the Las Vegas area, excluding downtown. Despite this, the name Paradise remains relatively unknown so, for this story, I'll continue to use Las Vegas, a moniker everyone knows. I am one of the rare breeds of people born in Las Vegas and have tolerated it enough to stay around for a lifetime. For visual support, I was born one mile east of the Stratosphere Tower and grew up in a house one mile east of one of Las Vegas Boulevard's most well-known resorts, Mandalay Bay, before it was the home of the Hacienda Hotel. In fact, the house I grew up in is now where terminal three of McCarran International Airport sits. The government bought my grandmother's house from her when I was a sophomore in high school, and we had to relocate. That address, 1126 Duke Johnson, was replaced by a community park, a rock's throw from terminal three. When I talk about my upbringing, there is no exaggeration in mentioning how surreal it was to walk into my front yard, hear the planes taking off in one direction and, in another direction, see the tips of the world's best casino-resorts. Before I was even a teenager, I would often bike parallel to the long stretch of road gluing together the most extravagant casinos, restaurants, nightclubs, and show productions. At one point during my teen years, I regularly attended the 24 Hour Fitness inside the airport. It was a ten-second car ride over. My dad would drop me off in the passenger pickup area, and I would walk in. I'd bet I was the only one who was not there for traveling reasons. I could access the main entrance to the gym right above the baggage claim area, a space where millions of international travelers navigated day in and day out. I like to put this into perspective for people, because I get asked all the time, "You're from Vegas? What is it like to grow up in Las Vegas?" And that's the perfect lead into my story. Today I meet endless string of tourists on the strip. This really is my backyard.

I met Amor one hectic September evening, over Labor Day weekend, on the Luxor Casino floor. I was doing some work there, and she happened to be staying there with a friend on what the British like to call holiday. I was quite attracted to the accent, even though I misunderstand some phrases; I decided I was going to do my best to understand this one. She was stunning and very passive. After the first few minutes of chatting, we settled into a calm conversation. I was ready to pull out my best tools to win her long-term attention. I was attracted to her physical beauty so, after a few words, I asked the only thing I knew best at the time. "Are you British?" Good one, Manny! (It was a wild guess, but I had met several over the years so I was confident.)"What type of nightlife activities have you been doing during your stay here in town?" I knew I would be in the driver's seat if there wasn't already someone showing these two beautiful ladies the best time here in Las Vegas. Pretty ladies get picked up quick in this town because promoters, hosts, big spenders, bachelor parties, are all quick to jump on inviting ladies out. Most girls have a full itinerary before arriving, but it was my lucky night. They were on their own, doing their own thing. I was going to do my best to sell her on allowing me be the guy and if she would let me, then I would also have a chance to get to know her on a deeper level. What are her interests? What does she believe in? Is she single? Has she ever been with a Colombian man who was born in America? I had this wonky idea that I didn't care where they (meaning the ladies) were from; if it was meant to be, it would work out somehow. For the time being, it wasn't even an issue to me that she was from the United Kingdom. You miss 100 percent of the shots you don't take—that concept trickled right into my approach with women at this stage in my life. I was wildly chasing women, every night. As we were engaged in conversation, I noticed things going very well, so I asked if it would be appropriate to exchange contact information.

Sure enough, she agreed.

"I am finished here in a few hours, would you like me to take you out once I am done with my work? I know a good entertaining nightclub, not in this smoky hotel, that's going to be busy this evening. You ladies might want to check it out."

"Sure that sounds great, we are going to hang around here in the hotel, maybe even check out the lounge here, and then let us know when you are ready."

"Absolutely!" I was so happy!

But by the time I finished my work and reached out to her, it was too late. Ugh! I was in need of some rest, because I was off to San Bernardino in four short hours to attend an electronic dance music festival with my friends. I was ready to go bonkers—for one day and one day only. Shufflin', jumpin', rollin', everything!

My weekend was shaping up to be fabulous. I was thinking, "I just met my future wife!" I was feeling good about our initial encounter. Now, I was driving out to the Ontario airport in California to pick up my best girlfriend, Janel, before grabbing lunch, having a few cocktails at the local restaurant, and then moving over to the festival grounds, fifteen minutes away. Janel had been my best lady friend for a long time; she's been through some shit with me and helped me in a lot of my darkest moments. Ring ring…ring ring…

"Hey boo! What's up?" she would answer often in the years before.

"What are you doing? I replied.

"At home, hanging out."

"Can I come over? I am cracked out, the boys are in town, and you know what that means!"

"Sure. You know you can."

"OK! Let's get some Chipotle! See you soon."

She was and is da bomb friend, and we loved this EDM life together. By sundown, we were already lost in the crowd, rubbing shoulders, sharing sweat, and smiling ear to ear because this was Nocturnal Wonderland. They call this place Wonderland for obvious reasons, and I can assure you I felt my mind, body, and soul disappear into thin air that evening and I never took a break. Well, except for the occasional water and bathroom break, which can take an hour because I was high as fuck, staring in every direction, taking it all in and stumbling through the choppy grass. Look out! Dodging every other raving person walking the grounds is another challenge, and it's a scramble baby! Have you ever taken a piss or shit inside of a porta potty when you are shaking, because the pills you just ate got you feeling like you are light as a feather, shaking, and feeling like a million fucking bucks? Goddamn that bass feels good on my balls! It's not easy! It takes some time, and don't forget the minutes it took me to go through my belongings, including a double check that I still had my drugs, always tucked under my nuts. Let's be real, men always were in charge of managing the drugs; at least in my time raving I had this responsibility. "OK. I am good." Back to the main stage to lose my mind some more. But this festival shit was getting exhausting for me. Still, at the end of the night, I smiled because I had an evening of laughs, shuffles, screams, singing along, getting high as the moon rocks—or is it just ate a bunch a moonrocks? Who knows, I am still high! With fists pumped, I shuffled some more, ingested moonrocks again, and captured the most invigorating moments on video. Watching my favorite DJs take the main stage was enchanting.

OK, it's time to switch gears. I was thrilled to head back home and spend the holiday weekend with my new friend, Amor. On the other hand, I was concerned, like a worried mother, because I had to drive straight back to Las Vegas after drinking, partying, dancing, and not sleeping for twenty-four hours. Thank God, I was still high and the energy was still flowing through my body. On the ride home, in the passenger seat, sat Janel, who was knocked the fuck out! "Well, I am on my own," I said to myself. She was an exhausted best friend by now, and she booked an early morning flight out of Las Vegas back to New Mexico to make it back for her scheduled work shift. Yes, we were that crazy. It was 3:00 a.m. by the time we got off the parking lot and on the highway back to Vegas. This was not the most rational thing to do, but I didn't rationalize too much back then. I knew I had both my life and my best friend's life riding on my ability to stay awake and drive us home safely.

We pulled up to my place just past 6:00 a.m. This gave us both enough time to take a quick nap, get up, get ready, and drop her off at the airport right before I would make my 1:00 p.m. shift. Most people call this type of action absurd, and illogical, but I would always do it anyway. I would always take myself to extreme lengths and test my limits. I always recovered, but darn if I didn't suffer many times over. Festival after festival, club after club, party after party, year after year, that was my life. Regardless, I made it back, safe and sound, and the rest of my weekend was ideal. I had the chance to spend some time with Amor and tune into a deeper, more personal connection, a feeling I missed and that had been absent since my previous relationship. It was a feeling that I so desperately wanted, something I didn't get very much of in my life. We both felt the chemistry, and we did our best to keep in touch and put our best foot forward at the chance of making this long distance lust a reality. This included plenty of Whatsapp and Skype until she would eventually come back and visit two months later. I was excited and uncertain at the same time.

Chapter 2
Cokeing Mechanism

"We all get addicted to something that takes the pain away."

—*Unknown*

A few weeks later, at the end of the same September month, I was on my way back out to Southern California. My two friends, Harold and Natasha were getting married. I love these two, they had been friends for a long time, and I had put them through hell, like most of the people who had been around me for an extended period. This includes the time a few years earlier when I was about to leave their asses behind at my house for EDC. "Harold, let's go! I am leaving!" I had no patience, and I'd be damned if I was going to miss the first DJ set. My car was sitting idle in the garage with music blasting. My excitement was high, but my nerves were on fire.

"Bro, chill out! My girl is up there getting ready." He yelled back at me.

"I don't give a fuck. I told you earlier that I was leaving at this time and you should have managed her better!"

"Chill out!" He said.

"No! I am not going to chill, you know how I am when it comes to this shit!"

"Whatever, just go then! Leave if you want." He screamed.

Now the others were getting uncomfortable because I was being an asshole and the negative energy was nasty.

The wedding festivities were scheduled to take place over three days. Day one—a party at the groom's parents' house in Rancho Cucamonga. Days two and three—we were moving our position down south, to the Hyatt Long Beach, adjacent to the convention center and downtown. I was in for a treat and completely honored to be included in the wedding, but the caveat for me at least, was that when a group of your closest friends comes together in celebration, there must be room for acting like a fool.

"Manny, this isn't Memorial Day in Vegas, bro. It's my wedding. Can you keep it together and just not turn up too much?" would joke Harold. I'm sure he was more serious than joking.

"Ah man, you mean no cociane or molly? Kidding. Dude, I'll be fine."

This group was used to seeing me at my worst, but somehow it would always just pass and nothing would be done about it. How could I let them down this time? It was another opportunity to compete with the boys on who could take more shots out of the bottle or a shot to break my record of how many lines of cocaine I could do in one sitting.

I sniffed, pushing the rolled-up one-hundred-dollar bill against the table, sucking up the white powder so hard that I could feel the stress on my brain…

"Ah!" I would shout in victory and gummy the leftover. This shit isn't cheap." OK! Minutes later I would say, "Fuck, my mouth is numb!" I became an expert at chopping the rocks and of organizing the lines with a California or Nevada driver's license. By line number six, in just thirty minutes time, I was getting such a fucking thrill out of how high I was, that six was only the beginning. Oh, sorry I get a little excited when I talk about drugs. Back to night one: Against all odds, I didn't touch anything. We finished off in modesty, as we gathered for backyard culture, acknowledgment of the bride, groom, friends, and family, and socializing.

On the second day, we woke up early and made the sixty-mile drive west to Santa Monica, cruising our way down by means of Interstate 10. Casual beach waves and beer, here we come! Santa Monica has long been my favorite SoCal destination. After my first road trip there in earlier years, I fell in love and, ever since, I never miss the opportunity to drop in, provided I have the free time during trips to Los Angeles. With its palm trees and crashing waves, the pier with large cones of ice cream and spinning carnival rides, Bubba Gump's with an ocean view, the Third Street Promenade, Barneys Beanery, Cabo Cantina and their delicious margaritas, and its boardwalk connection to Venice—it is the perfect close- distance escape for me.

After prancing around in Santa Monica, we had little time to check in and get ready for night two. Forty weddinggoers were loading up on a party bus, departing from the hotel valet, and cruising down the coastline to Huntington Beach, Main Street. The drinks were flowing on the ride over. The groom's brother stepped up and acted as the makeshift bartender.

"Manny Vegas…what are you drinking, bro?"

"I'll have a beer for now."

"A beer, that's it?"

As if they had no idea who this guy was who was only asking for a beer! God help me. Girls were dancing on the pole, centered in the bus, to the music mix of the bride and groom. "All right, this is cool. The party is jumping on the bus, and everyone is feeling good!" I thought. The playlist, in essence, was a collection of memorable songs that had a unique relationship with each family member or friend and how it reminded the future Mr. and Mrs. of each person. There were songs by Calvin Harris and old-school and new-school rap songs, all in the good spirit of keeping the party alive. The song they selected for me was "Work Hard" by

David Guetta with Ne-Yo and Akon. It was in 2013, at the Ultra Music Festival in Miami, where my friends labeled this as "Manny's song," so wherever we went, when the intro was identified, all eyes, smiles, and comments were on me. "Manny's song, Manny's song...," we would all erupt into our singing voices, "work hard, play hard," following right along, out stretching our crackling voices in an attempt to sound just like Ne-Yo himself. "Go, Manny! Go, Manny! *Go. Go. Go!*"

"Ah, shit...is this my time to turn up?"

I would say the first half of our ride was successful. When we arrived at Main Street and filtered into the bar, forty of us were ready to cause the bartender a stroke because there were maybe five people inside before our entrance. We were ready to wreak drinking havoc—at least that was my intention. I had just heard my song, had a good flow of energy, and what?

"They have fireball shots for how much? Did you say two dollars?"

"Yes, I did," said the bartender.

"Oh, Jesus!"

I don't think they were prepared for me, but surprise! I was used to shots being fifteen to eighteen dollars back in Vegas and, because we had two hours for dancing, I ordered as many of those sugary friends of mine as possible for myself and for others.

"Let's party! Now remember, Manny, this is wedding weekend," said that little annoying voice from the angel on my shoulder.

Could I handle this fireball freedom? Well, I didn't black out on the spot, but I opened up about my feelings with a stranger! I was getting to that point when the alcohol was turning me against my own silence; the truth serum was working it's magic. Booze would never prevent me from talking about what I was thinking or, more importantly, feeling. I was well on my way to blacking out at this point…

But wait…there's more to the night, and guess what? It involves me rolling around like a toddler on the tenth floor of the hotel after we arrived home, sniffing out some more of that native powder. I was pretty wasted by now, rolling around while trying to act coherent and talking on the phone with Amor. I was caught in action.

"Manny! What. are. you. doing."

"Huh? Man, I'm just relaxing, talking on the phone," I said, slurring my words.

Harold and his brother busted me. "Get up, dude. This isn't even your floor."

"It's not? All right, give me a few minutes."

Thank God, I was the embarrassing subject of yet another drunken snapchat.

"Manny Vegas, drunk, rolling around on the floor." Those were the relevant words as the phone recorded what some said reminded them of a stop, drop, and roll drill. Oh, yippee! Of course, I didn't care. I was off to rip a couple of lines.

"I need a bump!" I thought in my head. "Or several." I couldn't wait to get my hands on some cocaine.

After waking up from a few hours of sleep—go figure—resulting from the early morning snorting and drinking, I had already began to hate my life. I felt like shit. The obsessive shot taking and railing of lines had defeated me. And, honestly, I was still drunk, cracked out, and pissed off for doing it. The next morning is never a pleasant one. Nonetheless, I had to get my ass up and back to clarity because it was wedding day! My best friend, Ross, and I were rooming together. Ross had been sober now for a good period of time and had already spent one month in rehab following the engagement party we attended eight months prior for this same couple. He shared his opinion on the *choices* I was making and was slowly starting to affect the way I looked at my lifestyle. He shed light on the situation, the way-I-conducted-myself situation, that is, and he was now a voice of reason. It would be smart for me to listen to him. I mean we had been best friends for twelve years and destroyed city streets, our livers, and our minds over the years, partying, drinking, and using drugs. I am forever grateful for his health and his ability to get clean.

"You feel like shit, huh?" Ross asked poised.

"Clearly!"

"I feel amazing!" he says.

"Yeah, well, good for you." I wished I could have felt like he did. Somehow, with his morning encouragement, I was able to rally my brain and my body to get up for breakfast.

"Let's go grab some breakfast away from this hotel."

Where do you want to go?"

"Anywhere! Just get me out of this room, I need some fresh air."

It turned out to be a great idea to get my mind back on the right track. Coffee, fruit, and pastries did the trick in helping me feel slightly better because, throughout the day, we were all on high alert as the stress mounted in anticipation of the ceremony.

The day was comprised of getting outfits ready, the guys taking a crash course on how to iron the shirts, which I missed. And that led to.

"Are you kidding me? I just burned the fucking shirt!"

"That's what you get for trying to nap when his dad is showing us how to properly treat the material."

"Fuck, Manny, you hungover bastard, way to fuck that one up. Now you can't be in the wedding!" the groom says after I called him to break the news of my holey shirt. Umm, it was probably not the best time to tell the man about to get married that I just burnt a hole in my shirt, shirts that were custom ordered for us and the only extra one was for a man who was twice my size.

"Oh my God, what am I going to do now?"

Don't worry, the groom's mom came to the rescue just in time. Soon, there was added stress for being on time, followed by walking the groom out, sitting for the wedding, changing clothes, gathering for the reception, eating dinner, speeches, lines of cocaine for me, alcoholic beverages for most, dancing, more cocaine, more drinks, a change out of clothes, and then taking the party back upstairs to the suite. Phew, that's a lot! Did you catch that?

After the reception, most of the twenty-somethings were ready to elevate the night, but I was ready to lose my mind. Party time! "All right here we go!" I got excited. I was managing one very large bottle of whiskey upstairs, taking shot after shot from the open hole, holding it just below on the neck. "Ughhh, mmm, ahhh, that was rough!" a distasteful drink!

"You're an animal, who does that?" said someone watching me.

Within minutes, I realized I was boozed up and high on coke, not soda pop, but the powder again. I had made a commitment to Ross earlier in the weekend to drop him off at the airport the next morning, so I guess I had better slow down if I was to be alert enough to drive him up the freeway and then back home, 280 miles to

Las Vegas. Not even, I thought. Why not just stay awake all night? As the clock ticked, 12:00 a.m., 1:00 a.m., 2:00 a.m., the alcohol and drug supply was running very low and I was not ready for bed. I needed something to keep me entertained; I needed a backup plan. There were very few people still awake at this point. Logically, people go to sleep when they know they've had enough, but not me...

"I am from Vegas! And this is how we do it!"

Who the fuck was I trying to impress and why would this be beneficial to me? I was killing myself in some ways. One of the guys lived fifteen miles up the 405 Freeway in Hermosa Beach, so I thought it would be a great idea to go back to his place and keep hitting the booger sugar and drink some more.

"Yo, dude, do you have any goods back at your place? I'll pay you for it. Whatever it takes. I know you know someone."

"Yeah I do, wanna just roll over there?"

"Absolutely. I'll drive! Let's go."

We had two others who joined us. I mean, who was I kidding? Ross was dead asleep in the room. No more alcohol or drugs were available, so what's a guy to do? It made total sense at the time; albeit, it was a dumb-ass decision looking back. Could you imagine three more hours of drinking beer and snorting lines? It was four, five, six o'clock in the morning now. I was so withdrawn, I had lost track of time, only to realize that daylight was upon us. There is that annoying sun again, messing up my whole mojo! If my friend hadn't kicked me out of his apartment because he was getting tired, I would have stayed all day and forgotten about taking my best buddy to the airport. So the last three of us began making our way back to Long Beach. One was completely passed out on the ride home, but the other two of us were wide awake.

"Man, I am not going to sleep anytime soon."

"Me either. I could go for another twenty-four hours with the way I feel now."

"What do you want to do? I could totally go for some beer right now and just chill out in the lobby."

"Great idea, I'm in."

I parked my car at the hotel valet, and we wandered off into the downtown streets of Long Beach to find a store that sold alcohol. One block away, there she was a 7-Eleven that sold beer, the perfect way to end another bender of a night. Really, I was being fucking stupid at this point. People were checking out of the hotel, and we just walked in from the night with a twelve pack of Bud Light, pupils dilated, and cottonmouth. We sat our asses right down in the middle of the lobby. It was now when I realized my commitment to Ross, and I think this was the trigger to my comedown.

"I just got really tired," I said to the other dude.

"I have to drive home soon. This is not good."

The idea that I was running on no sleep made me incredibly nervous. What was I going to do? Call a friend and ask him or her if I could crash for a few hours? Sleep in my car on the side of the road? I didn't want to stay another night out here. Right now, I wanted to get away, as far away as I could. I had shot myself in the foot—again. There was no way I would be able to drive home without passing out on the road. I was in deep shit.

I said my good-byes, saw everyone off, drunk and high, and started driving to the airport. Five minutes into the drive I started to fade away. I even tried jumping on the phone with Amor. I didn't want to spill too many details about the night and proceeded with caution, because I was in fear of embarrassing myself. I was a complete clown for my decisions and actions. Either way, she tried to keep me awake and alert, but it wasn't helping. The strongest energy drink or even some more drugs couldn't have kept me focused and in between the lines of the highway. Thirty minutes in, I pulled over in West Covina, just east of LA, and settled in for the night at a local motel. I'm sure I would have either run off the road or crushed someone else driving along if I had continued the four hours to Las Vegas. And for what? To save a couple of bucks and time? Not worth it…I'm glad I made a smart decision here; those were rare.

Chapter 3
When the Fun Stops

"Insanity: doing the same thing over and over again and expecting different results."

—*Albert Einstein*

In August 2007, I was frantically trying to finalize a birthday surprise for my girlfriend at the time. Her big day was the second week of September, and I wanted to have the plans locked in so we could request the time off work and be well prepared. I pondered cautiously over likely destinations. I was still strapped for cash, so I had to be careful with my final choice. Room rates, drive time, spa prices, food and beverage cash, it was no "ball out" scenario, but I was trying to make her feel special as best I could. I considered Santa Barbara, but that was way too expensive, because I wanted to stay in a fairly luxurious hotel that wasn't a side-street dump in the form of a seventy-five-dollar-a-night motel. And in Santa Barbara that was how it was, so I didn't pick it. San Diego was a possibility, but that would mean a two-hour drive south, more gas money, fancy dinners, and a big-city budget. I was stressing over this idea. Stay in the Los Angeles area and have a fun local getaway? No. We were doing local activities routinely anyway.

Then I remembered the radio commercial I had heard not long before I started planning. "Pechanga Resort and Casino: Opened in 2002, Pechanga is California's largest casino, full of guest amenities— including a relaxing spa and resort-style pool to lay back and soak up the sun; entertainment lounges with live bands or your favorite music sounding through the newly updated speaker systems; a variety of restaurants to serve you; and fine dining from surf-and-turf entrees to casual breakfasts and lunches in the resort's cafe."

"Excuse me, but did I just hear that correctly?"

I was in another state, and this ad reminded me of something I had heard back home in Las Vegas for many years, with exactly the same pitch. They must have used the same marketing strategies, because the shit got my attention; or maybe it was the word casino, over and over again. I knew well how excited I got when spending time in the casinos. I was sold!

"Manny, you selfish prick, this isn't about you, it's about her. Duh, well I am still picking this place," went the dialogue with myself.

I called them up to inquire about our intended travel dates and, with ease, I booked the trip. The room rates were ideal. We could lay out by the pool and be entertained by the mountainside. The resort was in Temecula, about an hour and a half south of Los Angeles.

"Thanks for choosing to stay with us, Mr. Vargas."

"Ooh, she just called me Mr. Vargas," I giggled.

"Yes. Thank you for your help. Can you transfer me to concierge please?"

"Yes, transferring now."

"Hi, Mr. Vargas, We're happy you are staying with us. What can I help you with today?"

"Well, I want to organize a surprise for my gf."

I asked if the team could leave a roomful of balloons, chocolate covered strawberries, champagne, and a sign that read Happy Birthday laid across the bed for our arrival.

"Yes. Of course, we can arrange for that. Fortunately, we have a department with all of that stuff ready to go. I just need the name and estimated arrival time."

"You bet, her name is Clover, and we will be arriving late afternoon."

Before we left that day, I called, in obsessive fashion, several times to ensure all would be in the room when we arrived. I needed to be certain and bring thankful eyes when I opened the door after checking in. And to my enlightenment, everything was in place. Thank goodness. The stress was gone. Great job, guys!

I had earned my brownie points; that is, until the next day.

The following day, I had arranged for her to get a "you're not at work, take a breather" birthday spa treatment. I did not join, because I figured I could save the money and use it for something, anything else. Food, drinks…gambling perhaps. And that is exactly what I did. I had time to kill, and this place was loaded with money-sucking machines and tables.

"Come on, Manny, now is not the time. You know how this goes when you play. You lose every time, and you could ruin this trip."

I didn't have much money, either. I was barely getting by and already stretching my finances for this trip, always with this woman in tow. I had less than $1,000 to my name, and we still had one more full day here before heading west to spend time at Laguna Beach. I remember thinking to myself, "Why not? I'm on vacation. I'll have good luck away from home, Vegas," where I must have already lost thousands of dollars, and I was only twenty-one.

"Oh boy."

I went to the ATM and took out a total of $800! What on earth was I doing? At the same time my lady was upstairs being pampered, I was below her on the main floor, throwing away the only money I had for us to enjoy this trip. Fifty dollar hands—no luck. I bumped it up to a hundred dollars a hand several times and, ouch, that was painful…I got killed there. So, then, I scaled back, twenty-five dollars a hand, and this was not any better. I was losing fast! Did it ever occur to me that I should stop? That I had to fund the remainder of our trip?

The only benefits from this quick hour and a half were the very expensive drinks that got me highly intoxicated. And trust me, I needed the buzz. I lost all of the money in one fast sitting. I sat there and stared at the table, hoping my money would reappear, looking down at the floor in case I spotted a black chip the guy next to me may have dropped. To make matters worse, there was someone waiting to play. "Sir, would you mind getting up so the next person can jump in?" I was experiencing a moment of, "I am going to rob this place, right here, right now, hands up motherfuckers!" In slow motion, the idea ran through my head, and I could see the execution perfectly, but then it dropped from straight emotion and reached the frontal lobe. I shook myself back to reality, which amounted to addressing myself this way: "You piece-of-shit loser, now what?"

When she called me to tell me that she was finished, I thanked God that I had already paid the bill beforehand. Can you imagine how ashamed I would have felt if I had to tell her right away…"Umm, I just lost all of my money. Would you mind paying for your own massage? I know I told you I would take care of everything, and I mean it, but this time I couldn't control myself downstairs and lost. Sorry."

Well, this is exactly what I had to do, and I felt like a lowlife for good reason. She came out and I was distraught. Angry face, lips and teeth clinching, I was forced to spill the beans. She didn't know what to say. And I didn't expect her to say much. I had told myself over and over again, "I can't take care of myself and there is no way I can take care of her. Why did I do this? What is wrong with me? Now what?"

I had to figure something out, because my debit card didn't work after the max-out abuse of the last hour. Do we go sit in the room and look at the roof, or do we go sit in the restaurant and watch other people eat? I was such a jackass. I was totally selfish and in need of a brochure, you know, the one next to every ATM? I called my father to explain the story and ask for a pick-me-up.

"Yo! What's up, dad?"

"Nothing, boy! What's going on with you?"

"Well, I am out here at the casino, and I just lost all of my money. I don't have any to get back to LA, and I don't get paid for another few days. You think you could help me out?"

I always ran to him after fucking up. I tried my best to dummy up the story.

"Come on, son! Ah, man, you know you can't be fucking off all the time like this and come running to me. I am not your bank! You have to grow up!"

"I only need a few hundred dollars. I promise this is the last time! Please?"

The last time…yeah, right…

If the definition of insanity is doing the same thing over and over again and expecting a different result, than damn it, Albert is right. I was that guy, so I must be insane. I admit it! Years later, nothing had changed. In fact, it got worse, because I was around and in the casinos more often and earning more money. I had zero control over my desire to spend money and gamble. Eating out, alcohol and drug abuse, other stupid shit that left me no value, reined. Gambling meant blackjack on the casino floor, video poker at the bar, and rolling dice on occasion where seven out left a bitter taste in my mouth, whether I was scoping out the five-dollar tables at the Flamingo Hotel or jacking up my bets at the hundred-dollar table inside the Bellagio to feel like a boss. In neither case was I playing it safe. In fact, most of the time I was on the edge of losing my last few hundred dollars, and dipping into my fragile bank account where I was always getting negative balance notices after making a POS debit. You know the telephone machine that sits off on the side of the casino, not far from the ATM, for degenerates like me? The one that takes a thirty-dollar withdrawal fee on each transaction? The one that provides a receipt to take to the cashier cage for verification and collection of the funds? Yeah, that one.

I would always take out $200, $200, then $80 from the casino ATM because, by the time the five-dollar fees added up and I hit my limit, I would not be allowed to take out any more money. So, then, I would walk to the POS machine, take out another $400, two separate times, while drunk, and hope I could put it all down on one or two hands right away, and start to make a comeback on my already-lost $480 never-respected dollars. Boy, did that ever backfire on me.

In many cases, the famous words rolled off my tongue. "Lemme get a hundred. I'll pay you back later. Come on, you know I have the money." This would happen in begging fashion, aimed in the direction of my friends. My friends could tell anyone how often I would ask to borrow their money—hundreds of times. Whenever they heard this, they knew I was busted or needed money for a double down. I would be anxiously sitting at the table with a king face up, and the dealer showing a six. The dealer would go around, chucking the second pass of cards out, and there it was, one more king. I would waive my hand, signaling a "stay." I would have a twenty on a double down with several hundred dollars on the table. I would sit nervously on the edge of my seat, waiting for her to start her process, praying that the cards she flipped over were anything lower than twenty or above twenty-one. She would show a six, the ugliest card in the deck, and, "My gosh, the book says bust!"…Not for me. I would see five…"Oh, shit," I would say, "not a ten!" Then I would see two, two, two, and a four! "Are you shitting me?" I would scream at the top of my lungs. "You pulled a six card twenty-one to beat my twenty? That's horseshit!" would fly out of my mouth, surely resonating across the gaming area, and in anger as if it was the casino's fault. I was disgusted with myself, so why not push the blame? What a crappy way to finish the night that became, too. I would have no more money and would still be drunk. I always wanted to play more, too, but often it was, seven or eight o'clock in the morning. The sun was out, and I had to walk outside, get in my car, and drive home, miserable. Where was a gun when I needed one?

When I first dabbled with gambling, I had zero responsibility. And I mean it—none. I was living with dad and grandma, they were paying the rent and buying the food, and my car was paid off (until I had to "get cool fast" and bought that car while I was living in LA, another dumb move). Anyway, I played the game and always chased the losses. I also got a walloping thrill from taking the risk. In my mind, I would always be OK, because, in those moments, I knew I would go back to work the next day and make more money. The problem was, I would sell myself this story: "I will recover, it's just money, I'll be fine, money grows on trees." Family and friends constantly told me to save my money, put it in this or that account, that I'd need it for a rainy day. Sure…why would I save money, when I was convinced I would get rich quick off the same game that was designed to take money? There was no skill in blackjack or craps. Counting cards doesn't equal skill and I wanted to do what was easy. It was nothing more than basic elementary math and playing by the book. Everything was left to chance.

As I got older, I was unable to kick the desire to play. I had a paralyzing weakness, and it would show up way too often in a life surrounded by more responsibility. I had to find a way to make rent, pay the utilities, and pay down the other mountains of debt I had, while concurrently increasing my bets by manipulating my own mind. "I didn't have a problem, I'll stop someday," went the internal dialogue. "When does that day come?" Once again, I was certain that I couldn't lose. That was because I competed, and "competitors always come out on top." Well, maybe that happens in the sports world, where talent and dexterity are present, but here the rules haven't changed. The casinos were not built from winners. I was still a loser.

Today, I know why I loved it so much. I was a risk taker from the beginning. I was taking chances as a youngster. Life was a gamble for me. I had a very addictive personality with zero awareness of it. I stood as the oddball out, and this gambling pleasure, as bad as it was, allowed me to see immediate results on testing my luck. I didn't have to wait for the outcome to materialize for more than one minute.

In 2010, Harold and one of his buddies were on their way to visit from California. As usual, I got the call. "Waddupp, we're headed to Vegas. Are you ready?"

Oh, hell yeah, I was ready. This was what I live for! At this time, I was working in the nightclub and well on top of partying. Partying and I had a very intimate relationship. I had all of the connections at every venue in the city; you name the venue and we were walking right in—no line, no cover, always! For some time, I had felt like I was really cool because, honestly, that's all people used me for, and I was totally fine with it. People knew they had me as a partner in party crime—drinking, drugs, and gambling, if they were rotten as I was. One night, after the club, we played some tables in the casino and I borrowed a few hundred dollars from him. Are you surprised I borrowed money? Don't be. He accepted it. I said to him, "No worries, if I lose it we can go back to my place. I have a safe at home with a little cash in it." At the time I did and, in expected fashion, I lost his money. He was still in college, so I needed to go back home and refuel his bankroll so he could leave town with at least the money I owed him, and I understood.

So we made the drive across town, back to my apartment, drunk, to pick up the money. However, I wasn't just going to pick his money up and let a couple of friendly hundreds stare me in the face. I flipped through them, thinking to myself…

"One more run, Manny? You can. Why not? It's what you always do anyway."

"Oh, all right." I agreed with the silent voice speaking to me.

"It's you for crying out loud."

Jeez, what a devil of my own voice that is. I picked up several hundred dollars more and headed back to the strip to drop Harold off at the hotel. It was already morning so, of course, I hated myself, again, for the self-inflicted torture.

On the way back, I needed to get gas for my car because I was on empty. "Dude, I am going inside to pay. Can you pump the gas?" I asked. "Hurry up!" I knew what I was doing. I could have paid right there at the machine, but I wanted to walk in and slip one—just one—hundred-dollar bill into the slot machine. In the gas station! If he hadn't have shown concern over the amount of time I was inside, then I might have lost all my money before I even got back to the casino! One would think I was in the bathroom going pee, maybe got sick and threw up; or, maybe, I was just drunk inside the convenience store talking with someone, but none of these scenarios were the case. I got lost in the moment of playing blackjack on the slot machine.

"Manny! What are you doing, bro?" I turned my head quickly, caught and humiliated. "I had to."

"Dude, I have to go back; I have to leave soon" he said, so we went back after I lost another hundred bones. "You have a problem," was the thought he left me with.

I was making $6,000 a month and normally gambling twice a week, at least, and I would gamble more money than I was making. The fun definitely stopped. I was a loser yet again, and this time my friends were witnessing the depth of my problem, one that I had hidden for a long time.

Chapter 4
Like a Broken Record

"History has shown that from times of great distress are sown the seeds of opportunity, promise, and renewal."

—*Sameet M. Kumar*

I know my behavior got to be really irritating over the years. Eleven years' worth, to be exact. Repeat, repeat, repeat. How many times can you put up with a drunk, high, money-begging, asshole like me? We'd be out, and my people would have the thought: "Manny is around with his eyes rolling in the back of his head because he just swallowed two molly and it's now the forty-five-minute mark…I think it's kicking in."

Maybe someone became concerned that I would get sick or die. How about when I was in Miami, wandering aimlessly on Collins Avenue after downing a bottle of Imperial Vodka one New Year's Eve, leaving my cousin in the distance, and bothered, because he was somewhat responsible for my return to his home. Or maybe when a group of my friends were just trying to have a good time in Huntington Beach, during spring break in 2010, the first time I decided to try cocaine. First, though, I took several hits of weed and twelve shots of Jack Daniels. Oh, fuuuck…I was an emotional rollercoaster that night.

"Hey, dude," I spoke in the direction of another man while he was taking a pee in the urinal next to me. "Do you have any cocaine? I just tried this shit for the first time and I need some more."

"What did you just ask me?" he said, as if I was in trouble for asking.

Duh, Manny, you cannot walk around asking strangers for drugs! He pissed me off, though, and before I knew it, I was almost the reason for an all-out brawl on the block because he refused to keep me in his bar. And if you are trying to kick me out, then let's fight! This was odd because I was never a fighter; however, on this evening, I could very well have gone skinny-dipping in the Pacific Ocean butt naked and been OK with it. Oh, yeah…I did do that!

As for the guy who kicked me out, yes, he was the owner of the bar. I was all over the place. Who in the hell did I think I was? Alternatively, how about who in the hell did I think I was in the case of my ex-girlfriend? This is exactly what she was dealing with, and she had put up with it for three years! I was annoying all those around me, and even myself on occasion. Talk about being an inconvenience. I would be fine for a few days, sometimes a week, and then I would break the good behavior streak. If life used a noncriminal jail, I would never be released for good behavior! I was suffering in my own personal prison.

In October 2014, I had a friend, Jonny, coming into town for a bachelor party. He was bringing a group of strangers, his friends, but nobody I knew, and I was responsible for hosting them. I regularly entertained groups of visitors. Over the years, I had been fortunate enough to build many relationships and earn a lot of referral business in due time, working in the nightlife industry. He was also bringing his new lady, who I would be meeting for the first time. "Hope you don't make yourself look like a clown too much, Manny!" I thought. I met them up in their suite at the Aria. They had a beautiful room wrapping the corner of the tower and stunning Las Vegas skyline views. Monte Carlo, New York-New York, and MGM were in my left peripheral. When I walked in, the group greeted me one by one,

"Hey, Manny, my name is "X.""

"Yep. Nice to meet you."

"Hey, dude, how are you? I'm Manny."

"Yes! You are the guy taking care of us this weekend!"

"Why yes, yes, that would be me—looking forward to it."

And the next. "Manny! How are you? I've heard a lot about you! We are so fired up to be here, and thank you so much for helping us out and doing all of this for us," would say the bachelor.

And then I would reach into my pocket and hand him one bag of cocaine and one bag of molly. "Here you go. I know you were just as excited about this!"

"Ah, yes! Thank you again. Can I get you a drink?"

"Sure!"

I made my way over to the conference room and wasted no time in finding the rolled-up hundred-dollar bill to snort that precious white powder, which I brought. Let's get this party started! This was becoming a common theme, this "let's get the party started" thing. Herding a group of ten amped-up gentlemen and one lady was no easy task but, after a good time socializing in the room, we needed to get to the club, so I successfully rounded them up and made it clear we needed to get a move on.

The group wanted to try out Drais Nightclub, a beautiful place that sits on top of the Cromwell Hotel, twelve stories up, with gorgeous panoramic views of the bright lights to the north and south, and at the busiest intersection on the Strip. My job was more about managing expectations and helping them bypass all the gritty work that goes into dealing with nightclubs, assuming that was a foreign concept to anyone. I had the workings of years of good relationships around the city. We were greeted at Drais and we walked in—no problem. I arranged for us to have a main dance floor table just a few feet away from the DJ booth. Boom! Boom! Boom! The bass was kicking! Lights were blinding me as they danced on their hinges above our heads, and Helena was the DJ. I had never seen her before, but who cared. She was a pleasure to look at with that sexy red hair! Mmmm hmm. I was out and ready to start a party. The table was great, and the excitement started to amplify. The models with bottles arrived, and the molly pills were swallowed shortly thereafter.

"Do you want one?"

"A molly? Sure, why the hell not?"

One of the mollies I brought for the group, by the way. I was selling and then consuming the same drugs. Lucky me! But I was working. So what…I never cared. It was the last thing I remember from the evening. Sound familiar?

When my eyes opened the next morning, I was startled. I was staring out of a big window, overlooking the bright, sunny, late-morning sky, and the pool of the Aria. I was curled up in a fetal position and still in the same clothes I went out in the night before. "How the fuck did I end up here, and what the fuck happened last night?" I looked around to double check that I was in a familiar place. Thank the lord there were a few bodies passed out on the couches behind me, along with booze bottles and trash everywhere. It looked like a hurricane had blown through the room…and where was housekeeping? Yep, this was the same room I had met everyone in last night. What about the club, though? Did we have fun? And why do I have this aching pain in my hip? Holy shit! It's a bruise the size of a soccer ball, it hurts like a son-of-a-bitch, and it's all black and purple. Ew!"

"Can someone, anyone, please tell me the details of last night?"

Although it didn't really make a difference, because I wouldn't remember anyway. I was sure to hear some crazy shit, and I wanted to know how everyone's night went. But I didn't necessarily like what I heard next from the groggy boys.

"Man, we left the club early, around two thirty in the morning," one of them said, which by Las Vegas standards is early.

"Did we do after-hours?"

"No."

"Did we hit the tables and drink some more?"

"Nope."

"Manny, you were so drunk that you fell off the top of the booth and came crashing down onto the floor below us, a good five-foot fall on your ass. They were kicking you out, so we all decided to leave. You couldn't walk. I am not kidding, you couldn't stand up."

I found out that the bachelor carried me all the way home over his shoulder; out of the club, through the casino, into the taxi, through the Aria, and up to the room and into my chair bed for the early morning.

"You have got to be kidding me?"

They weren't, and now my bruise made a lot of sense. I did a good job, on the job, of being a clown. Hooray!

Now think of this. I had to recoil from the night, but I also had to find a way to deal with being single now. I was alone, and I was running around town like a chicken with my head cut off. But it was what I knew best. I was upping the weight on my misery through acts of stupidity. So what did I do? Yep. I did it again and again and again.

Two weeks later, the madness moved to the Cosmopolitan, and this time I knew the group of fellas who were in town. Good friends, if you will. Same shit, different day. We killed it all weekend. Pool parties, nightclubs, hot girls, the whole nine yards. And to my surprise, they left me their room for the final night. I was pleased with that. Earlier in the day, two of us met a few waiting ladies downstairs, one of whom I was really attracted to was located at the entrance of the west tower.

"Hi, ladies!" My friend led the conversation.

"What are you up to?"

"We're just waiting for some friends to come down. How about you?"

My buddy was on a mission to invite girls upstairs and have them help finish off the remainder of the drugs we had before they had to catch the Atlantic-bound flight home. The girls, unsure where they would stay on this particular night, made it apparent they wanted an offer.

"Are you ladies staying here with your friends?"

"No we are just visiting them, and we are not sure whether or not we are going to stay in their room or find our own."

"Well, you are more than welcome to stay with me this evening. This lovely friend of mine is flying out tonight and is leaving me his room. I have the goods, and were are going to have a fun night! Maybe even hit up the nightclub here. Feel free to drop by whenever!"

"OK. That sounds good."

Sometimes it really is that easy. Not always, but sometimes. Is it weird that I offered up my room to two complete strangers?

I love, love, love—Did I say I love?—staying at the Cosmopolitan! This is for one awesome reason. The party is all stacked straight up. Never has it failed to be an awesome time there. It's a newer hotel, more hip energy, with a young crowd that tends to stay there. The flow of the daytime party turned nighttime party turned after party back in the rooms ensures a great time. You never have to leave the property during the summer and the early-fall months because the pools are poppin' in the day! Somehow, on this night, after the girls came back up to the room, I was introduced to an Australian rugby player. They called him the LeBron James of the sport, down under, in Australia. I had no idea who he was and my new stranger, my roommate for the night, just so happened to be a friend of one of his best friends, blah blah blah.

However, they were huge consumers of cocaine. Because I was helping people find it, they asked me and, without any doubt, I became their go-to guy for order after order after order. These guys had no idea who I was, and that shows you to what lengths people will go to consume drugs, especially in Vegas if they are desperate and have been unlucky with other suppliers.

"Manny, can you call your guy? We are going to need some more."

"Yeah, no problem."

You bet, I was marking up the goods 300 percent. These guys had a lot of money and were throwing it at me, literally, just like the piece of shit I was. My fingers were active on this night with my dealer.

"Can you get me three hundred?" We talked in code so that he didn't risk the phone tap; 300 meant two eight balls.

"Fo' sho', where you at?"

"Cosmopolitan. Can you hurry? These guys are bugging the shit outta me."

"On my way."

Meanwhile in the club, DJ Carnage was spinning some dirty trap beats and, in between runs to the car to pick up more goodies and up to the room to take more shots, I was able to find a little time to enjoy the music and dance in the club. What I did not anticipate is the direction the night would go in the hours following the closing of the club.

"Hey bud, do you want to come up to our suite with us?" Said the sports star.

"Who? Me?"

"Yes, you."

"My buddy is with me, I don't want to leave him."

"That's fine, he can come too."

Was I about to get my ass kicked by a bunch of Aussies who were all high and drunk, or was this really a kind invite for me, the drug dealer? I got invited up to the penthouse, but, ah, I'd been there before. However, this group grew and ended up including three celebrity DJs who were also in town, at the club hanging out, and friends of the guys I was supplying. It was nice to know the dealer got an invite. Apparently, this was my ticket for the evening, to partake and fit in over the course of several hours where a bunch of grown, celebrity, rich DJs played grab- and slap-ass until the wee hours of the morning.

"Is this really happening?" My head swirled and I thought I was dreaming. I was in the penthouse, having casual conversations with some gentlemen who I loved listening to. They were responsible for the original tracks and the remixes, all the music was shit I danced to, and had lost my mind to, for years.

"Your sound is so unique! It kind of sounds like this other dude I love," I said, ecstatic.

"Ah, that guy's music is a copy. He steals. None of it is original," replied one DJ.

One DJ was telling me how they, his group, started the movement in a genre of EDM that so many fell in love with. I was drooling at the mouth over the information I was hearing. They were normal human beings just like you and me. They loved to party and goof around. How often they partied I have no goddamn idea, but that's none of my business after tonight.

I noticed that in all cases of my time in this business that I always thought actors, hedge-fund folks, and professional athletes were some superhuman aliens dropped down from Mars, but they weren't. Some were assholes. Some were kind. I feel I got the good side of the stick, through the personalities I have met over the years.

Anyway, I rocked out with these guys all night, bouncing back and forth between my room and the penthouse. Why? I don't know. To be honest, I was awakened the following evening, in my room, by a knock on the door.

"Knock knock...knock knock...knock knock knock," and then I could hear the card being inserted into the thin, door keyhole, and the mechanism processing the coding.

"Kfskdfnsjnfkin...click click...Hello. Mr. Vargas...Hello."

I popped up! "Yes, yes?"

Realizing I had no idea what had happened, blackout of course, I noticed the room was freshly cleaned and had been vacated by the girls.

"Sir, you can't be in this room anymore."

"OK, OK. I am leaving." I didn't even question the man.

I was scratching my head, wondering how I managed to sneak back into a room that I didn't pay for on this day and sleep until 8:00 p.m., and then housekeeping cleaned it! Honestly, it is still a mystery to me today; but then again, when I was that high and drunk, I realized anything was possible, and I mean anything. I didn't even have to change on the way out because I was still fully dressed and in my shoes. I picked up my wallet, phone, and keys, and walked out the door. And then I checked off another Las Vegas night in my growing book.

Manny, who doesn't know shit about self-control, kept insisting to his people, over and over again, that the best way to live their life is the way he suggests. Manny is not the guy to listen to, and he won't shut up.

His friends, surely questioning his advice, have told him he sounds like a broken record, and that they have no intention of listening to him when he can't get himself together. Manny is so big-mouthed that his friends are now considering leaving his ass behind when they do anything because Manny is a liability. Hopefully, Manny will read between the lines about what it means to be a broken record and change his behavior, forever...

Chapter 5
The Struggle Is Real

"The struggle of life is one of our greatest blessings. It makes us patient, sensitive, and godlike. It teaches us that although the world is full of suffering, it is also full of the overcoming of it."

—Helen Keller

I was sitting in on a seminar here in Las Vegas when the speaker says to the group, "There is value in the struggle, but don't stay in the struggle."

"Ooh, that's good!" I thought. "I like that one." Now, I don't have the slightest clue whether the speaker personally crafted the phrase, but it sure had power behind it. At least for me it did. I know from personal experience that I was terrified to confront the truth of all my challenges as I was staring them right in the face. I was more concerned about how I looked to others than I was about finding inward well-being. I did a great job for a long time at building my ego up on false premises, and found out the life I designed in such a way could possibly come crashing down at any minute if I was vulnerable in discussing my struggle and exposing myself to humiliation. I was inexperienced at facing my true feelings on any given day. On top of that, I was unable to manage my behavior because of the lack of self-awareness.

When I wake up every day and get dressed, I'm thinking, I am going to wear this for Jenny from down the block so that she will think my new white tee is fresh, Manny fresh. Or, I am going to post all kinds of selfies on Instagram seeking comments to make me feel better. Right? Because that's where we find our self-worth, isn't it? No! Or I am going to gamble to get rich quick, or drink to make the pain go away, or snort a line of cocaine because everyone else is doing it…

Oh honey, audit your alignment, the one that is the gateway to your best self. And if it's off, fix it! There is absolutely no long-term fulfillment in life if you aren't practicing extreme self-care and love.

We've all had those days. Like when you oversleep, which throws a wrinkle into the entire morning turned afternoon turned night—causing a frantic run around the house, trying to get the kids dressed (if you have kids) and the lunches and coffee made for later in the day. Not to mention breakfast, but maybe the kids we're already up and noticed you were behind so they helped you out and made bowls of cereal for themselves. In any case, thank them, or whoever is there for you next time, for being of service.

"Oh my God, the world is ending," most say, looking at the chaos around the house, and it might not even have been twenty minutes. You are so far behind, and it's a good indicator of how the rest of the day will play out. Once you get to work, your boss is frustrated that you are late, and clients are waiting and forming a line that fills the hallway. You catch all of the nasty nagging. And finally, finally, lunch has come and you get a break, but the boss barges in and tells you that it is not happening because now you must play catch-up. "Why me? I hate my life…"

What do you do next? The day sucks at this point. Do you make a decision to give it a meaning wherein you are totally responsible for its failings, or do you say that it's a onetime mishap and learn to turn it into a positive? Do you ask for forgiveness, ungratefully, and grieve about how you survived yet another bad day, a day full of struggle? After all, it is normal for us to have heavy workloads, families, all kinds of responsibilities. Or is it? It all depends on how you choose to filter it, but I can tell you this much. When you decide to stop playing the victim of your own pity party, you might start to witness the dawn of a new day, maybe even of a new life. If you are one for whom this has been happening routinely, then you must do a serious evaluation on your life. Ask yourself, What the hell am I doing? And what do I really, really want?

If you are thinking that your life has turned into one big rut, and you find yourself continuously thinking about it so much that your body becomes tense, take a deep breath and come to the reality that you need to do something about it. But where do you start to find a solution? There you are, stuck and living on the edge, waiting for the tipping point.

What are we supposed to do when the struggle is real? How do we transform our lives? If you are anything like me, regardless of the individual event, you want to get out of this cave. Badly. My suggestion is to go searching for the wisdom of your heart, and ask yourself questions that spit back positive answers. It worked for me—ask and you shall receive. When I woke up that November morning, with Amor looking at me mortified and skeptical, it was time for me to start asking myself questions. I was fed up with my life, and the results I had had up to this point. I wasn't interested in living a life of struggle anymore.

We had just come from an amazing vacation to Los Angeles and Laguna Beach. In a matter of five days, we did almost everything you can in the Los Angeles area. It was Halloween weekend, and we stayed right at the bottom of Runyon Canyon, a beautiful outdoor recreation area I lived near during my brief time in LA. I knew Los Angeles very well, and it was my job to show her all of the great features of the city. It was her first time to the coastal city, and she had every reason to be excited.

"Oooo, oooo, I want to show you the Hollywood sign first!"

As we were entering downtown Los Angeles on the freeway, we looked up at the green signs labeled "Hollywood."

"Ok! I am following your lead," she said.

The Hollywood sign was our first stop. We drove the curved hillside streets to get an up-close and personal experience with the landmark and the Hollywood Hills. Lake Hollywood Park was impressive.

"Oh my gawd, it's so pretty here," she said with awe eyes.

The sunken park fit nicely into the hillside and proved to have gorgeous views, with us, standing there, taking it all in, from every direction.

"I think that's Brad and Angelina's house! And there is Rob Dyrdek's! Have you ever seen Rob and Big? They lived right by Lake Hollywood!"

"Nu-uh! Shut up. How do you know that?"

"Because all I do is watch TV!" I said, acting like the know-it-all.

At nightfall, we were back in our rented apartment, dressing up and smooching, getting ready for a walk over to Hollywood Boulevard for a King Tut–themed Halloween event.

"How do I look? she asked.

"Now you are one sexy pussy!"

She was dressing as Catwoman, and I had worn my outfit from the wedding a month before. Very original, huh, Manny? I had never been to Hollywood Boulevard during Halloween, but it looked like New Year's Eve in Times Square or on the Las Vegas Strip. People were everywhere! Drinks, cuddling, and dancing made up most of our time there.

"Are you having fun?" I asked.

"Yes."

"Are you? No doubt, I replied. I am loving the way this trip has started. Want to get out of here and head home to have some fun? Rawwwrrr."

"Let's go, you dork."

Although we didn't stay out too late, it was a great finish to the first day of our trip. By the way, we didn't have sex, I was too tired and fell asleep. Womp, womp, wooooomp...

The following morning, we walked the canyon from the bottom to the top.

"We started from tha bottom, now we herrrr!" And then all the way back to the bottom. Damn, it was pain on the legs.

"What do you think? Isn't this gorgeous, Amor? Come here! Take a look at this...look at that, there is the Hollywood sign again but from a different angle."

"Oh my gosh. I need to take a picture," she said.

"Of course. I love this canyon. I used to live right down the street and would come here every day when I lived out here. I instantly fell in love with it, as I did with most places in LA. But the clear skies and the view! Oh my God, the view is wow."

"How do you feel?"

"I'm tired," she replied, with heavy breaths, and I was in no better shape.

"Yeah it's exhausting. How about we head down and relax, clean up, and then head to the beach?"

We were staying two blocks down, and it took us one minute to get home. I booked this place on purpose. After cleaning up, we jumped in the car and drove the city streets.

"Do you want to see popular destinations? Rodeo Drive? Maybe we'll catch a shopping Kim and Kanye. Sunset Boulevard? Have lunch at the famous Saddle Ranch? And then head to the Venice Boardwalk? There we could walk the few-mile stretch, lined with out-of-this-world sideshow acts showing off in front of Muscle Beach. Ooh, my buddy said we should try Abbot Kinney, too! Are you still with me?"

"Um, yes. That was a lot!"

"Oh, sorry."

After wearing out the tread on my car tires from driving, we happily sipped two- for-one margaritas at Cabo Cantina on the Third Street Promenade. Yes! I was back in my favorite area. Might I add, these margaritas were so damn good and, by the time a nice buzz was settling in, I took a look at my phone to check the time.

"Shoot! We need to get going soon! Nooo, I don't want to leave." I said in a baby's voice.

She didn't mind so much, but we had evening plans. "Check, please!" I paid the bill and, as we walked out, we couldn't help but notice the sun setting over the ocean so we ran over to the edge of Ocean Avenue, and stood at the edge of the cliffs overlooking the multicolored ocean. The reflection of the sun's rays was breaking through the cumulus clouds, thick in their presence. This view was a photographer's dream. The pictures we got together were priceless.

"OK, OK. Now we really have to hurry home. We have a long drive back to Hollywood, and we need to freshen up and make it over to the world famous Laugh Factory Comedy Club on Sunset for Chocolate Sundaes. Are you ready to laugh your ass off? I questioned.

"Ha-ha." There, I just laughed. She was funny.

"Wiseass." I commented.

As you can see, we had already learned to have fun with each other. Jokes were included, which seemed to relieve the tension for a first road trip. Sure, our minds were running wild—we all know how this works. Does he shower before bed? Does she brush her teeth in the morning after waking up? Does either person snore at night? Because if so, then this definitely is not going to work! Does he fart in his sleep? Oh, please no, I don't think I could handle that. Does he put the toilet seat down after taking a pee? He better, or I am catching the next flight out!

On day three, I made plans for us to visit my friend at his waterfront beach house in Oxnard. These were our last few hours in the Los Angeles area before journeying back south to Laguna Beach for the remainder of our time in California.

"Do you want to drive through Malibu on the way back? We can take PCH and split the spine of Malibu, so that you might get a sense of where the movie stars of the world have a home away from home. Why was I trying to show off these places? Because I needed to prove myself. Plus, it's lush, ocean on one side and earthy mountains on the other."

"Sure."

My gosh, she was so simple and I admired that. She was just there, living in the moment. We made a few coastal stops where we pushed our backs and feet up against the small waves flirting with the sand.

"Look how close the water is to us," she smiled after I said this. "I've been out here a few times and, on occasion, they say you can see the dolphins a couple of hundred yards out having a party in their large pool."

There was no party that we could have the pleasure of witnessing from a distance this time and, by the time we arrived in Laguna Beach, in late afternoon, we were wiped out. But the hotel featured gorgeous ocean views from the rooftop balcony. There was no way we were going to nap; there was not enough time to capture the remaining moments, so we boiled up what energy we had, went upstairs and ordered some margaritas, and sat comfortably underneath the blankets we dragged out from the room. It was the perfect combination of sight and sound, staring out at the expansive blue sky and listening to the waves crashing on the shore every ten seconds.

Everything we participated in during this trip was intensified, because the time spent far surpassed what I expected and, to be frank, neither of us knew what the hell we were getting into. We were just living all out, the best we both knew how to up to this point. It was only two months earlier that we met, in Las Vegas, and now we were on vacation, still strangers in time calculations, despite our frequent long-distance communication. "This is risky business," I would think periodically.

On the first night, we pleasantly joined my friends David and Collin at a local restaurant, Nick's. David was a very good friend of mine over the years and helped me through some of my deepest shit times. I am forever grateful for his kind heart. Why not see the boys if they are around and available? Nick's was rated a go-to restaurant on Yelp, and the reviews were accurate. They had delightful food and drinks. We all enjoyed one another's company and saw to it that Amor felt comfortable around more strangers, who just happened to be my friends. She was a quiet lady on this evening, and I couldn't tell if that was because she was uncomfortable or because she was shy. I hoped it was the latter, but I never found out. I mean, she came home with me and she didn't fuss, so I'll live with that. The fine wine and cocktails were the ideal sleep-solving formula. "Good-bye to you gentlemen. It's time for us to get some rest." So we returned to our hotel, one minute away, and fell asleep comfortably, side by side.

In the morning, we were fully charged. The sun was shining baby. "Let's get up and go walk around. And lay at the beach. It's our last day of this California dreamin' vacation. Now feelings were starting to get involved. There were moments of excitement and there were moments of sadness, because I knew our time together was coming to an end. Soon, Amor would be back on a plane, flying over the globe, home to the United Kingdom. Anyway, I had to remove those thoughts and treasure the last day we had together in Laguna. Across the street, I saw an Urth Café.

"Let's go there!" I screamed with excitement.

Urth Café was a famous establishment from Laguna's friendly neighbor to the north, Los Angeles, often seen in one of my favorite HBO series of all time, Entourage.

This day was a day of…Nothing. But. Relaxing…and we did just that. Our hotel was on the north corner of the main beach, so we had convenient access to a multitude of laidback bars, plenty of beach sand, and rocks, if we dared be even more adventurous and climb around. We started at a beachside bar, drinking mojitos, other fruity alcoholic drinks and, as I sat there, I couldn't help but eavesdrop on the table behind us—four intelligent men, with superb vocabularies, discussing ten million dollar oil deals. I figured it was a standard conversation in Laguna Beach. I mean, the residences in the hills remind me of what I see in the Hollywood Hills and Malibu.

"Ready to hit the beach?" Like two kids, we wandered down onto the sand and found our laying spot, spinning around like a dog before taking care of business.

"Here?"

"This is good."

"Booyah! It's relax time!"

"Can I bury you under the sand?" She was pitching me something I wanted nothing to do with.

"Huh?" I replied without wanting to acknowledge the question.

"Can I bury you in the sand?" She said again.

"You want to bury me in the sand? Why?"

"Because I think it will be fun."

"How?"

"With my hands!"

"What?" I thought she was crazy.

"Yeah, I said I want to bury you in the sand." She was serious.

"Yeah, right! When?"

"Now!"

"No!" I wanted nothing to do with it.

"Fine," she said.

I felt bad because she was just as excited as a toddler, and I couldn't bear the disappointed puppy-dog face.

"Fine! OK, OK, you win! Bury me in the sand, but I am going to read my newspaper. And stay away from getting sand in my mouth! I'd rather not have crunch-bite all day!"

"Hahaha," she laughed. Like she was ready to bury me alive...

"Oh shit. What did I get myself into?"

She wanted to experiment. It was worth watching, to see her get the joy out of it. She had me at this point. I wasn't just giving her my physical body; I was becoming vulnerable to her. The circumstances were irrelevant, though. In my mind, she was the best, and I'd do anything with her, and for her.

On the drive home, it was difficult not to reminisce, laugh, and enjoy our last road-trip car time, together. It would be the last time she and I would ever be in the same car again, driving from one city to the next. Two things were on my mind. How successful our trip was together—I can honestly say that I was wrapped in the astonishment for our five days; and, second, how, on the last evening of her stay, I got to show her how I party in Las Vegas. Undoubtedly, I was ready to showcase the life I lived, with her by my side. And maybe, on this November evening, I showed her everything she didn't want to see.

The second half of that night faded away, much like the scene in the movie The Hangover…

You get a brief glimpse, and speed through a sequence, of the night, the excitement, the drinking, the companionship, the drugs, the foolishness, and then…the frame takes you curiously through the flickering bright lights of the Las Vegas Strip. From evening and dark skies, to sunrise and quiet anticipation and, sadly, as we know it, the next day is unfortunately upon us. For many, it becomes a life-changing night of stupidity. Movie scene or not, this was my life, and the struggle was real. I was doing this all of the time.

I use this five day trip as my pivot point because of the emotional impact that fateful evening had on me, leading up to the transformation of my life. In the preceding chapters, I have told all. There are no more secrets, and it took a lot of courage. There you have it. You know my flaws. I have spilled the beans and opened up with all of my heart. If I didn't get control of my life back, by understanding the depths of my troubles, then, certainly, I would be forever chasing lost love and a spectacular life, just out of my reach. The struggle of nearly thirty years, bottled up, just like the longneck Bud Lights I had been buying for the last decade. It was time to open the top and free up the liquid inside.

We all have a responsibility to be true to ourselves. Yes, this means that if you have a problem, seek help, better yourself, and drop the idea of embarrassment. If going straight to the doctor, seeing a therapist, or hiring a coach is scary, then take baby steps. But without taking some sort of interest in the improvement of your mind, body, and soul, life will get the best of you. If you do the things in life that are easy, life will be hard, but if you do the things in life that are hard, life will become easy. I heard this from the world's best motivational speaker, Les Brown. And he was absolutely correct. I had to come to terms with my issues. I was worth more. I was better than this. And I'd be damned if I was going to keep living this way. It was time to change my life around, and nothing was going to get in my way.

PART TWO:
THE DISCOVERY

Chapter 6
Check the Gauges

"A good system shortens the road to the goal."

—Orison Swett Marden

So there I was, the day after my last and final episode with drinking. I was also giving up drugs...no more drugs! Damnit, Manny, you should have listened in elementary school, to D.A.R.E. I wanted nothing to do with any mind-altering substance that would affect my brain chemistry anymore. I was forced to take a step back and ask myself, "OK. What's next?" I only knew an adult life of partying, and now I was setting sail into the open sea, with no clear destination. All I knew was, I wanted better for myself! And, I wanted to get as far away from this destructive lifestyle as I possibly could, not by running, but by confronting the issues at hand.

After working down a list of my problems, I asked myself the first question. "What is the centerpiece for me behaving like this?" I needed to know if there was a common thread linking everything together. And, of course there was. It was the alcohol. Each time I would drink, the drugs, the gambling, and the tyrannical behavior were omnipresent. On this day, I made my declaration of independence from alcohol. *No more alcohol!* There was no other choice. This was now a must in my life. Sorry, booze, but it is time for you to go. Would I be able to stay true to the demands of myself? Would I be able to resist all of the temptation? You bet your ass I would, and I was out to prove it to myself and the world.

Three days later, I was required to be in the office for a staff sales meeting. It was a Monday morning, and I was on my way in to hear the owner of the company. He was going to give us a presentation, or attempt to cheer us along in our efforts, and try to motivate us for lasting results that stick—so ri-ri, ra-ra, for both the company and for ourselves. I sat in, having survived three days of not taking a drink. It was too soon to use the word sober, but I was free from alcohol over the past weekend. I was feeling refreshed when I entered the meeting. We all sat in the conference room and, as I looked around, I could see each person in the room looking miserable for having to being there. It was one of those meetings where you show up because you have to be there, not because you want to be there. In fact, for me, it was the first meeting I was attending. My boss was kind enough to move it up a week for me, because I had been out of town the week before on my vacation so the timing was great. The meeting was a perfect follow-up in relationship to my new direction in life. It must have been God shining his light down on me, saying, "Here you are, son. The world is in your hands now." And it was confirming my decision to stop the drinking and drug use.

Chris, the owner of the company, walked into the room. He was a very friendly and successful guy. And then, everyone suddenly stops talking, as if he or she will be punished for making a peep now in the man's presence. He is the foundation of this office and responsible for $15 million of business, which pays all of us. His signature is on the checks. So, remember, I had only decided to stop drinking a few days prior, which means my brain still works the same; no severe changes had yet been made. For the most part, I am still the same ol' guy with the same thought patterns at this point. I am still a long way from my desired best self, but I had made a decision. I had a goal, and I was after it.

I thought I was the "know it all," or "the guy in the room who believed he was ahead of the game," that is, until the lights went down and the projection of a famous clip appeared on the wall, from the movie Boiler Room. Ben Affleck delivers a speech as the character Jim Young. In case you're unfamiliar, it goes like this:

Okay, here's the deal. I'm not here to waste your time. Okay? And I certainly hope you're not here to waste mine. So I'm gonna keep this short. If you become an employee of this firm, you will make your first million within three years. Okay? I'm gonna repeat that. You will make a million dollars within three years of your first day of employment at J. T. Marlin. There is no question as to whether or not you'll become a millionaire working here. The only question is how many times over. You think I'm joking? I am not joking. I am a millionaire. It's a weird thing to hear, right? I'll tell ya. It's a weird thing to say. I am a fucking millionaire. And guess how old I am? Twenty-seven. You know what that makes me here? A fuckin' senior citizen. This firm is entirely comprised of people your age, not mine. Lucky for me, I happen to be very fucking good at my job, or I'd be out of one. You guys are the new blood. You're gonna go home with the kessef. You are the future big swinging dicks of this firm. Now, you all look money hungry, and that's good. Anybody tells you money is the root of all evil doesn't fuckin' have any. They say money can't buy happiness? Look at the fuckin' smile on my face. Ear to ear, baby. You want details? Fine. I drive a Ferrari 355 Cabriolet. What's up? I have a ridiculous house in the South Fork. I have every toy you could possibly imagine. And best of all, kids, I am liquid. So, now you know what's possible. Let me tell you what's required. You are required to work your fucking ass off at this firm. We want winners here, not pikers. A piker walks at the bell. A piker asks how much vacation time you get in the first year. Vacation time? People come and work at this firm for one reason: to become filthy rich. That's it. We're not here to make friends. We're not savin' the fuckin' manatees here, guys. You want vacation time? Go teach third grade, public school. Okay. The first three months at the firm are as a trainee. You make $150 a week. After you're done training, you take the Series Seven. You pass that, you become a junior broker and you're opening accounts for your team leader. You open 40 accounts, you start workin' for yourself. Sky's the limit. Word or two about being a trainee. Friends, parents, the other brokers, whoever, they're gonna give you shit about it. It's true. $150 a week? Not a lot of money. But pay them no mind. You need to learn this business, and this is the time to do it. Once you pass the test, none of that's gonna matter. Your friends are shit. You tell them you made 25 grand last month, they're not gonna fuckin' believe you. Fuck them! Fuck 'em! Parents don't like the life you lead? "Fuck you, Mom and Dad." See how it feels when you're makin' their fuckin' Lexus payments. Now, go home and think about it. Think about whether or not this is really for you. If you decide it isn't, listen, it's nothing to be embarrassed about. It's not for everyone. Thanks. But if you really want this, you call me on Monday and we'll talk. Just don't waste my fuckin' time. Okay, that's it.

I watched on the edge of my seat, fully attentive, and listening to this twenty-seven-year-old young man get straight to the point. It was a movie, sure. But the content, the content was, oh my gosh, "I want to be just like that guy!" I was ready to get up and move mountains. I was fired up! But how could I do all the great stuff he was talking about? Remember that spirit I was unsure of, beneath the surface, waiting to burst out? This is it. Your true potential is buried in there. You need to find the keys to unlock the cage so it can express itself. Minutes after the clip was over, Chris stood up and opened up the room for comment.

"What are your thoughts are on the short clip?"

Everyone had a point of view, but I kept silent. My mind went into overdrive. I was more concerned with what I was feeling inside. Give me more! Running through my mind were thoughts of absolute power…and then we got to the reality. With a marker in hand, standing at the whiteboard, he began to ask us questions.

"What are you doing to become better at your job? How are you putting yourself in a position to succeed? What are your goals? How are you allocating your time?"

Chris tells us he gets up in the morning and watches a "TED Talk or motivational video," much like the one mentioned above. I didn't even know what a "TED Talk" was.

"Who is Ted? Jesus, Manny, you don't know TED Talks?"

"The little bear that I laughed at in the movies? Mark Wahlberg's Ted ? Is that Ted?"

I knew about motivational videos, but I was disinterested in watching them because I thought I had all the answers. But, I mean, if this guy was doing it, and he's suggesting to kick the day off in this fashion, then I had to drop my arrogant attitude and give it a try. If he had the money and the free time to live a life that I was after, why shouldn't I give it a shot? Anything would help me at this point. My mind opened up out of curiosity.

Here I am thinking, "I've got this, I have an answer to these questions." It was so not true. In fact, I couldn't have been further from the truth. I wasn't dedicating myself in any way toward being more successful. I was just going through the motions. The best definition I've since heard for success comes from Earl Nightingale. "Success is the progressive realization of a worthy ideal." The key words here being *progress* and ideal, or *goal*. I had none of these until a few short days before. I certainly had none set up for my work or my finances.

The truth was in writing on the board. Chris pointed out…

There are twenty-four hours in a day.

You work x hours a day, say eight. Now you have sixteen left.

You sleep, if you're average, eight hours a day. Now you have eight left.

If you have kids, you take care of them one hour a day, if not more. So let's say two.

Now you have six hours left.

Let's think about the time you spend eating breakfast, lunch, and dinner. I'll be kind and say one hour. Now you have five hours left in the day.

We haven't even gotten to the part where humans, on average, watch five hours of video content each day—TV, the Internet, movies…

Do you see where I am going with this? Before you can blink your eyes, your day quietly disappears. You are one tick closer to the end of your life. I shit my pants when I got the picture. I was doing everything he wrote on that board, every day. And I somehow fitting partying into it. How in the world could I expect to be successful if this was my way of spending my time? Time I can't get back. It was gone. I was on a path leading to land of the hopeless. It was time to take a personal inventory to see which shelves were empty.

Here is what I discovered.

- I discovered that I was directionless.

- I discovered that I was a procrastinator.

- I discovered that I was not my number one priority.

- I discovered that I needed to change the way that I was thinking.

OK. I had had enough of the meeting. I got what I needed. It was a reality check, and I took away an understanding of how to better adjust the blueprint of my life and start to shape the life I wanted. For starters, I was going to go back home and pull up the TED Talks listed on Netflix. But wait. That was TV! Well, in this case, it was valuable video content, a channel of information to which I would soon become addicted. It was a start in a new direction.

When I got home later in the evening, I was thinking over and over about what was said to us in that meeting about time. *"Time, time, time."* I knew I was stuck. But, because I was curious to know more and try anything, I opened up a TED Talk on Netflix and started to watch it. By the end of the night, I had watched five, consecutively. I found myself interested in something other than Narcos, which was a darn good series. Could it be that I may had just identified a new hobby for myself? I think so! And it was actually stimulating my brain, which seemed to accept the new idea.

Once I became aware of what was really holding me back, and where I actually was standing in relationship to my current, crappy position in life, I was able to make a decision. It was clear: A decision to keep going down the same unproductive, unsettling, and unforgiving path, or a decision by which I would grab my life by the throat and say, "Now I'm in control, and we are out to get better!"

It was time for me to create new law and order in my life. All the broken rituals that had been consuming me for years just weren't cutting it. I had a new starting point now, and even though I didn't know where I would ultimately end up, I was doing something to get unstuck. YouTube was great. After I watched the TED Talks on Netflix, I went to the computer and started doing some basic searches on more TED Talks. In between finding a list of additional videos, there were also suggestions on the right side of the page, usually related to the video I was watching. Without noticing, I was carving out a new process to my life. I took the advice of Chris, and used his suggestions. I was feeling quite different about myself, and within days, because I rarely took and advice from anyone, much less implemented it, my time was becoming more productive. After making a few simple adjustments, I loved it. My life's lease was about to expire on 911 I'm Stuck Rd.

Over the next several weeks, I would be challenged in every possible direction. Fresh from making a firm decision to stop drinking, the waterfall of friends came pouring in. Both friends I knew and strangers I was now making new friends with. Complimentary drinks were part of my social lifestyle. Each time I was offered a drink, I deferred with confidence. I was getting used to being out and expecting people to try to pressure me, but I was also expecting myself to say no. As the time passed, it was getting easier. My new discipline was working. I learned that if I told myself I was going to do something and didn't do it, then I was lying to myself. That wasn't fair to me, and that's not OK. So I knew that if I couldn't follow through, I wouldn't agree to do it, for starters. Baby steps!

One evening about two weeks after my decision, I met another woman. Two women actually, but one of them caught my attention, of course. Right? I met her on the casino floor of the Cosmopolitan, next to the Henry Restaurant downstairs. I approached her aggressively and, to my surprise, she was very responsive.

"Hi, listen, I watched you give me the eyes back there, and I couldn't help but come and introduce myself. What's your name?"

"Kristen."

"Nice to meet you, Kristen. How is your evening going?"

"Great. We are just trying to see what to do next."

"I am getting ready to head up to the Marquee Nightclub. My buddy Kerry works the door. You are more than welcome to join if you'd like!"

"Yeah, why not."

I love when people are friendly. I was soaring on a new life and taking every new approach with women I could, just because I felt a slight increase in my spirit and confidence. So I ended up taking them upstairs to the Marquee Nightclub.

"Kerry, wasssup my man? Just a few of us here."

"Yeah, no problem, come on in," he said as he gave us several free drink tickets.

"Oh no, not for me, ladies, these are for you."

"What about you? You aren't drinking?" They asked me.

"No, I am free from drinking for a few weeks now. I am trying this new style of living out."

They nodded and said, "That is awesome—good for you. I wish I could stop drinking!"

People wanted to stop, but they didn't know how. Life was getting cooler. I could now turn down several free drinks without the notion of trying to impress a woman. A huge improvement. I was doing it. I was staying true to my commitment.

So when you find yourself unsure of where to start in unwinding, try these simple suggestions...

– Acknowledge all your shortcomings and become aware of all your past misfortunes. If you have sucked at life, then just tell yourself: I have sucked up until now. No more will I suck! Finding yourself in the now, and identifying that there is a problem greater than you, is a great starting point to take control of your life again. (or for the first time if you have never had possession of it). Accept your weaknesses and all the results your life has brought you up to this point. But remember, the past does not mean that it will be your future. Wouldn't it be great to keep your health? Your family? Your relationships? Your money? You can have it all, and the choice is yours.

- Take inventory. Check all your inner shelves and see what's in stock and what's not in stock. If you're running low on understanding your emotions, pull up Google and check the Internet for some answers. Identify what types of actions you are taking on a daily basis that get you "x" result. You want your actions to drive you forward, not backward. We have access to all of our inner workings at all times. Be honest with yourself. Please stop bullshitting yourself on false premises.

- Create a process in which you assess the actions from above and streamline them. Create a step-by-step process by clearly stating what needs to happen from start to finish in order for each action to yield you positive results. We want positive results! Write them down. I strongly encourage a journal. This portion of the process also suggests that you think of contingency plans for any adjusted action. If the first one doesn't work, it is always rational to have a backup plan.

- Consider what types of tools and resources can help you get your result in a more efficient manner. Think about saving time and using leverage—doing more with less. Any successful person will have mastered the use of leverage.

- Take action! The gap between what we know and what we do is the difference in achieving what we want or not achieving what we want. We are all wonderfully blessed with infinite knowledge, but applied knowledge is what sets the winners apart from the losers. It's time to take what you have learned and will learn and do something with it. Use it. Abuse it. Step by step. And watch your brain power rule.

– Invest in yourself continuously. I don't mean take your money and put it into your 401(k); there is nothing wrong with that, but I am talking about something completely different. Take your dollars and invest in continuing your education, whether you are twenty years old or sixty years old. You are never too young or too old to keep on living the learning life. Buy books, attend seminars, watch online video, buy programs. There is a wealth of information out there, and the minute you surrender your learning you might as well call the mortuary.

– It's your turn to breakthrough!

Chapter 7
3x Diet

"*If it doesn't challenge you, it doesn't change you.*"

—*Fred Devito*

Whenever I write, I look for inspiration through my intuition or the universe. I let the ideas come to me and, when they pop in, I greet them. I was thinking about how I wanted to start this chapter before I went to bed one evening. I turned to my mind for the answer over a night of sleep—maybe I would have a dream and then wake up with the thought ready for use. But when I woke up a few hours later (this night I couldn't sleep much), there was no thought. I didn't have the answer I was looking for. So I proceeded with my normal morning routine. I pressed play on YouTube, which was up in my computer window, danced to the playlist to get my morning energy at a positive frequency, and then ate my oatmeal with berries, banana, and protein powder. Ironically, when I sat down at my desk to do some reading twenty minutes later, an advertisement sounded up through the speakers. I heard something out of this world!

"Freedom is at the edge of your couch watching TV…"

What the hell? Who is responsible for this madness of an advertisement?

Consider the following diets I used for my personal transformation as you read the remainder of this book:

▪ Newsdiet

Did you buy that advertisement? Sadly, people are influenced by mass media, whose job it is, to brainwash us. They paint colorful pictures, doll up products, and sell them in real time. Does your reality look like this? If so, there may be severe consequences.

Imagine you are in bed, watching the nightly news on ABC, and notice that after the news anchor blows through a list of the suicides from the day another headline pops up: "Possible terrorist attack threat for the upcoming Memorial Day weekend." You are instantly sucked into the monitor. And you start up a conversation in your head. "Oh my God, I am flying to New York this weekend, Jimmy is in Las Vegas with his friends, and Amber is backpacking around Europe. Oh my God, oh my God, please tell me this isn't true." On any given day, your mind starts to spin like a top. You begin asking questions, talking to the TV—and the media is pretty good at mindreading, because somehow they answered your questions before you could even speak out loud. "Well, where is the threat? Is it red, orange, come on! Tell me tell me!" Those damn news reporters…

We are overwhelmed with information that affects our daily lives, attention, and our personal identities. Maybe you pick up the latest edition of Us Weekly, and the normal Kourtney Kardashian and Scott Disick drama is covering the front page in fascinating style. "Kourtney and Scott…Is It Over? "Kourtney Hooking Up With Justin Bieber after Getting Cozy at the Beverly Wilshire?"

Now your own concerns surface. Is my relationship OK? Am I being cheated on? Am I not good enough? How could they break up? They have three kids together! Newsflash: Why are you so concerned with someone else's life, and not yours? That is poisonous information, designed to activate the brain in a way to make you a consumer. So how about this? If you are going to be a consumer, why not be one in the best interests of yourself? Buy a book on how to become more aware of you. Attend a workshop where there is human interaction. Try an audio program on personal development, late night, before bed, instead of listening to a news anchor talk about the seven murders and holiday terror threats. The keyword here is threats. Threats build fear. Do you get what I am saying? Fear and brain suicide are two weak takeaways from this particular information. How do you win in this case?

You might believe this was the worst day of the year so far. And just like we have 9/11, a day to remember, we should also have a single limited day of terrible headlines, at least the way the news media positions it. After all, it's inner suicide listening to this crap. Here are some additional headlines from various news sources from the same day:

"Trump for President": If you're not a Trump fan, your whole day flips upside down.

"Obama Vacations in Hawaii": Is he not allowed to spend quality time with his wife and kids? After all, he is human like the rest of us. And he has basic human needs: love, connection, and significance, to name a few.

"The World's Most Expensive Yachts Cruise the South of France": This one really makes you feel like you're missing out.

"The San Andreas Movie Kills It at the Box Office": Oh, man! Let's go see it. But I live in California and I'm terrified that the giant wave is going to submerge San Francisco with the next quake.

"Apple Refuses to Pay Taxes in Headquarters City": Oh my God, they are such a bad company, but I still buy all of their products.

"The Economy Looks To Get Weaker": Thanks. We are already concerned for our jobs. This makes me feel way better.

"ISIL Takes Control of New Territory": Do they have control of you or your thoughts?

Then there's the quick fifteen-second clip on Tony Robbins, saving a group of nuns in San Francisco. That doesn't matter as much? And the tiny piece in the back of the newspaper on how we can feed more under privileged families? Why doesn't that doesn't get as much attention? Shouldn't these last two be at the top of the list and on the front page all the time? Where are the stories documenting the journey to success? Where are the stories about how one heroic man jumped in front of a car to save his kid? This stuff is happening every day but, sadly, the stories are not featured in as wide of a display. The media knows these types of pieces don't fit the interests of the majority.

If you think that turning the channel to watch Game of Thrones, or flipping through your social media feed to check who's posting what is important, then you need to stop and think. Am I benefiting from this move? What am I learning? Does this show really deliver good value? Are my Facebook friends really my friends? Or do I just have eight hundred people on my friends list, 99 percent of whom I never talk to? Am I more concerned with entertainment than I am with achievement? You know the answer. Tell the truth.

"Oh, shame on you, Manny! Shouldn't you be a little more conscious of what is happening in the world? How can you serve people if you aren't aware of the pain and suffering happening across the globe?"

This is my response: "I need to feel at my best, first. If I feel alive, and well, with lots of love to give, and full of good energy, then that helps the people closest to me by the process of osmosis. The population is made up of individual human beings. If my energy is out of this world good then, by law, it infiltrates the psyche of all those around me."

Can you see the affects you are having on other people? Be useful from energy of a positive source. Do not engage in down-sided brainwashing or brand-washing. Instead, brainwash with harmonious thoughts—giving thoughts, helping thoughts, or becoming-a-better-person-for-mankind thoughts. The more people working on their own happiness as an inside job, the more the positive results we will get for the greater good of the people. Spend 95 percent of your time on a solution and only 5 percent on the problem. News is 95 percent problem and 5 percent solution.

Listening to news anchors talk about terrorism isn't going to get terrorists to stop blowing up planes, buses, or buildings. It isn't going to stop a guy from walking down the street and robbing a house. Stop putting fear into your mind through media scare tactics. Worry about being the best you, and I promise the world will become a better place.

If you choose to be a fan of the news, try these tips to control the madness.

—Pay attention to how the news affects your mood.

—If you're a news addict, find the positive news and focus all of your attention on that content.

—Declutter your information stream. Get rid of the bad. Open up for the good.

Here is a fun exercise.

Start with one day, then five, then twenty and establish progressive goals—don't watch any news, read any gossip magazines, or channel surf. You can and will find more productive things to do in spending your time. Natural curiosity will begin to show its face and take you on a new journey. Try it, and trust me, I have done it. This is from personal experience. Whenever you feel suckered into checking in on the outer world, stop and think first of something inside of you, the you that is better than tuning into negative news. Instead of feeling sorry for some situation you have no control over, try to be grateful for a situation happening to you right now. Give yourself a chance to break old habits and build a new ones. You'll be thrilled with what you discover.

• Friendsdiet

Just as important as it is to drain the bad media information holding your joy hostage, is ridding yourself of all negative people and energy, "friends" included. I have a real appreciation for people because they are humans and children of God. Everyone is blessed with unique gifts and talents. But we all have our troubles, too. Once you set off on a new journey for yourself, you will learn that some people you once had close relationships with are not on the same path as you anymore. And that's OK! If you outgrow your "once upon a time" best friends because you are on the rise, then you have nothing to feel bad about. Believe it. New, more stimulating relationships will start to enter your life.

I heard this eye-opening statement not long ago. "Let's say you were traveling by air, and the plane suddenly started to experience a decrease in cabin pressure. The oxygen masks are released. Yours does not come down, but that of your friend, who is traveling with you, does. Does he or she offer you the mask? Or share it with you? Do you take turns getting air? Or does your friend selfishly use it only for him or herself?" Hmm…This got me thinking. I know, through my own transformation in life, that I have watched people attempt to sabotage my growth along the way because they became envious. Whether they were doing this intentionally or unintentionally, it was just the path they were on.

This category of people, who are often our friends, with whom we often spend the most time, are the ones I file as "off my frequency now" friends. They might be against your progress for any combination of reasons. Maybe they fear you will exit their lives if you become so awesome they can't keep up. Or possibly, though they haven't told you, they feel your enthusiasm and new outlook on life makes them insecure. Who knows? Or simply they could just be scared of change. In any event, it is your job to know what you want and where you are going. And if anyone stands in the way, sorry. I still like you, but I have to spend my time working on me. While you are here talking to me about being broke, I should really be spending time reading a book on how to create wealth. While you are sitting here talking about how bad your job sucks, I should be focusing on how I can be the best at mine. You owe it to yourself. You are worth more than someone dragging you down is. Do you see the difference? If you have four broke friends, you will be the fifth. If you have four lazy friends, you will be the fifth. Catch my drift...

"Don't let someone who gave up on their dreams talk you out of going after yours," said Zig Ziglar.

The consequences of this cancerous attachment work hand in hand with some of the most common emotions: anger, resentment, and frustration. When you least expect it, and trust me, it is daily, negative attitudes damage your opportunity to become better. They diminish your happiness, personal growth, and opportunities to succeed. Noticing the patterns in your inner circle and coming up with a constructive way to step back from them is a self-awareness skill, viable to your development, health, and happiness.

For many years, I was the guy everyone came to know as Manny "Vegas." This meant that my closest network of friends had only one impression of me: that I would be there right alongside them for any party, festival, restaurant outing, or bar-hopping night on the town. I knew how to have fun, and my friends knew that. Heck, that was all I knew. But when I pulled back from that lifestyle, I thought it was wise to alert them of my new path in life. But it also became very apparent that, if I wasn't going out holding hands with them for these occasions, then they were not interested in keeping contact as much. We were going in different directions at this point. Once again, this is congruent with the process of a spiritual awakening. *It's your call on how you want to manage your friendships and assign values to them, but I caution you to pay very close attention to the inner workings of the relationships and how they are benefiting you, if at all.* Remember, you only have to look out for yourself. Because at the end of the day, you have yourself to hold accountable for your failures and your successes.

▪ Junkdiet

Every time I see a fast-food commercial, I start drooling at the mouth. McDonalds, Wendy's, Jack in the Box, all have the most tasteful, well-executed marketing when it comes to making their burgers, fries, chicken tenders, and milkshakes look like a million bucks. They do such a great job that, before I took control of my eating habits, I was the first one to get off the couch, put my shoes on, and head to the drive-thru for the latest version of the triple-angus beef patty, with onion rings, Monterey Jack cheese, and dripping barbeque sauce…or any other new menu item. I still have the occasional craving, and I do pop in once in a while. But once I felt a turnaround in my health—including my mind and body, as a result of dropping the salty fries and fatty patties—I was on the feeling-great and looking-better train. I say better because my body is a constant work in progress. I have to work hard to maintain my health. It does not just happen by pure luck or chance for me.

My exposure to junk food started when I was younger. I remember it was a celebration to stop at McDonalds or Taco Bell and dive into a super-size number one with a Coke or Taco Bell's savory gorditas, saucy chalupas, and sexy burritos. I would wake up my dad early in the morning, and beg him to take me to Burger King for a five-piece french toast sticks meal, and I was a little kid.

In case you didn't know, kids always find a way to get what they want. It might take a little bit of crying but, as any parent would agree, sometimes it becomes too much. So they say "screw it," let's get you that ice cream you want. The more I reflected back on my life, the more I became aware of what was happening at each stage of it. In my younger years, I'll be honest. I was a porker. Maybe it was all baby fat until I got into high school, but that's no excuse to munch on all things salty, fatty, and greasy. I can remember walking around the schoolyard, very conscious of my protruding belly, and taking my shirt in between two fingers and pulling it off my stomach so that there would be air between my belly and the shirt. This would work to avoid having the true shape of my center staring the other kids in the face and generating an unwanted laugh.

When I got into high school, I was years into aggressive athletics. I was a full time baseball player, playing year round and traveling. There was no lack of activity during physical education class, either. So it doesn't surprise me that, when I went to high school, I hit my noticeable growth spurt and lost a lot of weight. Over these years, it seemed impossible to put any muscle on. However, as my baseball career started to get more serious, so did all of the additional activities, including diet and weightlifting. I was never a serious weightlifter; I always did just enough to gain some strength and then maintain it. The problem: I couldn't get the idea of a good diet down. I assume now that I didn't give a rat's ass and had the teenager attitude of "ah, no biggie, I'm young, and I'll be fine."

In high school, the cool thing to do was organize get-togethers, head over to the local taco shop or diner, and buy all of the ninety-nine-cent items that were available on the menu. The comical part: I had not started drinking yet. There were no sloppy drunk crusades for late-night meals, at least not yet. I didn't start drinking heavily until college, because in high school, I thought it was unhealthy for me to drink and play baseball. Strange. But for some reason I thought it was permissible to eat like crap and be an athlete. Now, the more I think about it, the difficulties I experienced in catching my breath during sprints and the mile runs were because I was always opting for junk food.

In college, I was already a natural junk-food eater and an undisciplined weightlifter, and I was about to add drinking to the mix. I don't even have to say much else, except that there were many late, late nights over the next twelve years, leaving countless fries on the top of my driver's seat, leftover burritos in the refrigerator, and bellies full of Jack in the Box to fall asleep with. Alcohol and junk paired up. No wonder I was always burnt out, exhausted, and lethargic. Then I started to notice, when I wasn't at peak performance (which was more often than not), that I would start to feel emotionally weak. I was turning out to be one unhappy, junk-food eating, alcohol-drinking, skinny-fat man.

In college, grandma and dad weren't around to cook, and the campus food wasn't your traditional egg whites and spinach with chicken breasts, so you settle. You just go with the flow and deal with it. I can't remember many people taking full control of their diets; many people at this age are in their prime fitness years, and they can get away with eating like bottomless pigs. True story. But, as they say, it will catch up with you. And it did me. Overworked and with no self-control, I felt my physical and emotional health start to deteriorate over the years. I always used the size of my stomach, and the flabbiness of my love handles, as a gauge on whether I needed to make an adjustment, and one fast. I'd pop in the gym and do two solid working weeks, then return back to lazy, normal, unhealthy eating. I couldn't find any consistency.

At the beginning of my transformation, I took full control of working out and my diet. I didn't know how to follow a routine, and I knew little on lifting weights the correct way, but the more I listened to audio programs and motivational videos, the more consumed I was with the mind-body connection. I desperately wanted to get my mind on the right track, and if I could give it a boost by eating healthier and working out more often, then count me in. I would wake up in the morning and prepare for a morning workout. Sometimes, I went to the gym and ran on the treadmill for two miles, or I would sit and bike for twenty minutes. Other times, I would drive down to the local mountain and listen to Tony Robbins walk me though a morning procedure. Everything he said to do, I would do. It was getting real clear to me that, if I wanted to heal my mental challenges, I would need to take care of my body equally.

Tony would say, as I listened to his YouTube videos, "The fastest way to change our state is by physical activity—change your physiology— movement and change. Develop ongoing discipline— we are our rituals." This was a new ritual for me, and I was trying to develop it. He also said, "Create a set of physical rituals you won't miss—three, four days a week," And he also mentioned that, "in order to transform:

1. Feed your mind.

2. Condition your body—It gives you strength to follow through when your mind gets tired."

On top of Tony's advice, I had recently heard some fascinating stuff on happiness from the documentary Happy, and that material said to "seek out experiences that release dopamine," relating that the best way to do this is physical activity. It makes you happier. Oh, really? I will be happier if I do more physical activity? Ok!

As motivational speaker Zig Ziglar would say in his online video recording, "Get involved in an exercise program, the mind and body are one. Activate your pituitary gland that activates endorphins. This is 200 times more powerful than morphine, it floods the system with endorphins, and gets you on a natural chemical high. Energy-vitality-creativity." Zig added, "a healthy body equals a more alert mind and mental attitude."

OK, so now I can do physical activity, feel happier, and feel like I am on drugs without even taking drugs? Count me in!

No fitness trainer would have been able to get me to buy into this but, because I wanted to get my mind in order, and these guys were always on my computer screen via YouTube videos or talking through my headphones during my exercise activity, I was all ears and applying these concepts daily. I learned that, in order to optimize one's mind, one must get his or her physical body in shape through physical activity and eating healthier. Then watch long-term health flourish. Also, I was going to save a lot of money.

I decided to do a full-body cleanse, concurrent with my new exercise routine. I went to my fridge and dumped out all of the fattening crap: bread, chips, cheese, and the late-night (or midday) pit stops at the local fast-food joints. It was not just a small decision; it was time for a full makeover. I was treating myself like a porta potty at Coachella, shitting all over it. I had seen one too many of those gross bathrooms, and I was not about to accept my body being treated as one anymore. I went to the store and bought all of the salads, fruits, and oatmeal available. I was a new, healthy person, and it felt strange. I had gone through a restoration without alcohol in my body, so how could I not also adjust and adapt to the no-junk-food diet? I did, and I was feeling better than ever.

The more I realized these two concepts needed a marriage (and also understood that no diet is perfect), the more I was succeeding at coming into a new body and mind. I understood the work and the discipline it takes always to live in a high-performance state. The most fulfilled and successful people on earth, almost always, incorporate some sort of exercise routine into their daily activities. Most use their first waking hours to get a comfortable workout in before even looking at an e-mail. It's a fresh and mind-clearing way to start the day.

I was lazy, unhappy, and out of shape, though, and it was turning me sour. Without the adjustments in my daily routine to become a more active and healthy individual, I would not be as content with the direction my life was heading. I began using the mind-and-body connection to my advantage, with an appreciation for those who inspired me to make changes after decades of unhealthy dieting. Here are a few things I now constantly do and pay close attention to.

- Get adequate sleep. You are not helping your health by killing yourself to make a deadline.

- Run or walk outside with exposure to sunlight every morning within thirty minutes of waking up. This will get your endorphins and brain activated to prepare you for a productive day.

- Find time to work out forty-five minutes a day, again, preferably in the morning. But if you can't find a routine that works and stick to it, hire a trainer for some extra push in the first month.

Chapter 8
Call It What You Wanna Call It...I'm a...

"Surrender to what is. Let go of what was. Have faith in what will be."

—*Sonia Ricotti*

Whenever I would hear someone talk about alcoholism, or an individual being an alcoholic, I would think to myself, "Wow, that must really suck. What is it like to have a craze for boozing? It can't be that hard to just say no." I was uneducated in my reasoning.

Do alcoholics wake up and take a shot, first thing, after getting out of bed?

Do alcoholics think about drinking a whole bottle of tequila after work to calm down?

Are alcoholics hiding how much they drink from their significant others because they are embarrassed that their honeys might come up with some radical assumption and leave for good?

Or are alcoholics dealing with some tragic loss from childhood that makes day-to-day living too difficult?

In any of these cases, the alcohol and drugs are often used as a coping mechanism for something much larger than just the pleasure of being a social user and scoring a buzz.

I will never forget the day I went to my first AA meeting. My aunt, Danielle, swore by the program, because she completed the twelve steps and had been sober for a decade. My best friend was now sober and also a fan of the process. She insisted that I go to a meeting and test the system and to see what kind of impact the program could have on the alcoholic who still suffers. How about the new guy, the new-to-the-program alcoholic? Me, I was thinking to myself. "Why I am going to an AA meeting if I'm not an alcoholic?"

It was a sunny, mild Thursday afternoon, and we drove across town for a meeting in the Del Webb area of Summerlin, in the Las Vegas Valley. I was nervous to be quite honest. I didn't know what to expect, and when I walked into the room I was shocked to see I was the only young man. Everyone was double my age. I'm not kidding, they were all senior citizens! "How did I end up here?" I asked myself. Well, because the location was in a retirement community! Go figure. Now it made sense why everyone was twice my age. For being a first-timer, I remember thinking, "Well, I am scared shitless right now, but I have my aunt with me, and she did a good job of giving me an AA briefing. OK, let's see it all in motion."

The room was packed, so we sat in the rear. I looked around and thought, "All of these folks are alcoholics? That can't be possible." I needed to hear more. My attention was focused, and I wanted to make some assumptions about the state of mind of the people sitting in the room. But who was I to judge? I quickly learned that those people were suffering. Immediately I started to feel empathy, and I still didn't know anything about the program.

Here is how it works, a system that millions of people have followed, a system that has allowed many alcoholics a second chance at life. It was read as follows in the meeting.

HOW IT WORKS

Rarely have we seen a person fail who has thoroughly followed our path. Those who do not recover are people who cannot or will not completely give themselves to this simple program, usually men and women who are constitutionally incapable of being honest with themselves. There are such unfortunates. They are not at fault; they seem to have been born that way. They are naturally incapable of grasping and developing a manner of living which demands rigorous honesty. Their chances are less than average. There are those too who suffer from grave emotional and mental disorders, but many of them do recover if they have the capacity to be honest.

Our stories disclose in a general way what we used to be like, what happened, and what we are like now. If you have decided you want what we have and are willing to go any length to get it—then you are ready to take certain steps. At some of these we balked. We thought we could find an easier, softer way. But we could not. With all the earnestness at our command, we beg of you to be fearless and thorough from the very start. Some of us have tried to hold onto our old ideas and the result was nil until we let go absolutely. Remember that we deal with alcohol—cunning, baffling, powerful! Without help it is too much for us. But there is One who has all power—that One is God. May you find Him now! Half measures availed us nothing. We stood at the turning point. We asked His protection and care with complete abandon. Here are the steps we took, which are suggested as a program of recovery:

1. *We admitted we were powerless over alcohol—that our lives had become unmanageable.*

2. *Came to believe that a power greater than ourselves could restore us to sanity.*

3. *Made a decision to turn our will and our lives over to the care of God as we understood Him.*

4. *Made a searching and fearless moral inventory of ourselves.*

5. *Admitted to God, to ourselves, and to another human being the exact nature of our wrongs.*

6. *Were entirely ready to have God remove all these defects of character.*

7. *Humbly asked Him to remove our shortcomings.*

8. *Made a list of all persons we had harmed, and became willing to make amends to them all.*

9. *Made direct amends to such people wherever possible, except when to do so would injure them or others.*

10. *Continued to take personal inventory and when we were wrong promptly admitted it.*

11. *Sought through prayer and meditation to improve our conscious contact with God as we understood Him, praying only for knowledge of His will for us and the power to carry that out.*

12. *Having had a spiritual awakening as the result of these steps, we tried to carry this message to alcoholics, and to practice these principles in all our affairs.*

There I was, sitting in the room, thinking to myself, "Whoooa! What just happened?" I still couldn't settle in, but these folks were convinced these principles worked. Still nervous, I had many ideas running through my head. I wasn't sure if I was more nervous about having to speak standing up in front of the group and talk about the idea of being an alcoholic, even though I didn't know why; or that I heard twenty short stories of life experiences from people who have done things just like me. After an introduction and some informal discussion jumping around the room, I quickly realized I was not alone. The twelve steps were saving precious lives. And some who were still finding it difficult to cope would always find their peace by following the twelve steps. While others were sharing their stories, I sat there, saying, "That sounds like me...Yep, that was me one day...Oh my gosh, I did that?...No way! I have felt that before...Blackout and throw-up everywhere—sure, many times...Got aggressive with my ex-girlfriend...That's true."

Everyone was the same and suffered from the same illness. This group was using the one and only system proven to help alcoholics find their purpose in life. If you spend enough time in meetings, all you will hear is how much better life has become after getting involved in this program, and that if people ever got off track, it was because they got away from the program.

At the end of the meeting, I was swarmed by the group—a celebrity style ambush. Maybe they thought I was Elvis? That was more their time. Nonetheless, these people were friendly and supportive. I had the chance to interact with a very kind group. They were by far the most receptive group of adults I had been fortunate enough to cross paths with. And I have dealt with hundreds of thousands of people. This was an energy, a way of living, that I was unaware of. These people were here to serve their fellow alcoholics; they put others first. I walked away with more phone numbers and books than I could have anticipated.

"Call me if you need anything. I am here for you. Come back and see us every week. Do you need a sponsor? Make sure you read the big book and the twelve steps."

"Oh crap." I was overwhelmed. What was happening? The environment was very peaceful and more supporting than what I was used to. They included me. They made me feel connected.

I started going day after day, trying new locations, and meeting new people. Every time the response was the same. "My gosh," I was thinking, "everyone needs to attend an AA meeting, alcoholic or not. It would make the world a better place."

On my fourth straight day of meetings, I got to the bottom of it. I still had no clue what it meant to be an alcoholic. I had been hearing about this great scripture and reading material, and paying attention to heart-touching stories, but I couldn't make sense of why I was here. So, slightly embarrassed and very hesitant, I turned to my aunt and asked, "How do you know when you are an alcoholic?"

She looked at me and said, "Well...it is when you're powerless over alcohol and your life becomes unmanageable—step one."

I looked at her, eyes wide open, and instantly started to recall every single time that I drank alcohol. I was exactly that! The blackouts, the gambling, the drugs, the driving drunk. How could I not notice? I didn't know. I wasn't educated on the disorder. I was too egocentric to believe I was an alcoholic...but no! I was. I had just been informed why, and I couldn't hide from the truth anymore. In this moment, I admitted to being, surrendered to being, and accepted the fact that I was, indeed, an alcoholic. For over a decade, alcoholism took full control of my spirit, the results of my life, and I was blind to it. I had to swallow all of this, right now, or I was screwed. I had been obsessed with destructive drinking. And I had been frightened to admit it for fear of feeling like a coward. In fact, I learned that, for many alcoholics, it takes time at first to come to terms with the idea and wholly accept our state of untreated alcoholism or drug addiction. At this rate, I had a triumphant weakness, with a large probability for loss of life. I was living and dancing on the edge of a cliff with no safety harness. Unfortunately, for those who fail fully to surrender to the ongoing, unstoppable, and sometimes fatal diseases of alcoholism or drug addiction, the fragile, intoxicated mind can take a backseat and forgo staying in control, leaving one restless. These restless minds are frustrated, impatient, and unhappy, often times leading to more excessive drinking.

"Who cares to admit complete defeat?" This is the question asked in the twelve steps and twelve-traditions book. "Every natural instinct cries out against the idea of personal powerlessness. No other bankruptcy is like this one. Alcohol now becomes the rapacious creditor, bleeds us of all self-sufficiency and all will to resist its demands. Once this stark fact is accepted, our bankruptcy as going human concerns is complete."

"But upon entering AA we soon take quite another view of this absolute humiliation. We perceive that only through utter defeat are we able to take our first steps toward liberation and strength. Our admissions of personal powerlessness finally turn out to be a firm bedrock upon which happy and purposeful lives may be built."

It was just then that I gave myself to the universe. I was done with trying so desperately to fit in, to cope with twenty-five years of loss, and to fly high in clouds of arrogance. It was my turn to take a deep breath and relax. It was my turn to have all my dreams calmly become one with me. I had been pushing all my opportunity away with both arms extended. And for what? There was no satisfaction in the taste of alcohol. I wasn't helping myself accomplish my goals. My health, wealth, love, and happiness were all deteriorating because of my alcoholism. The clarity fairy showed up, circling above my head, dumping all of her dust kindly upon me, saying, "You are in control now. Do as you wish." The pressure of ten thousand bottles of vodka was released immediately.

I had to adopt a new attitude, a new way of living. I had to keep absolute faith in myself that I could be anyone I wanted, do anything I wanted, and live the life

I always wanted, not the life I had been faking for many years. Because I knew I was making the right decision, I started to trust that everything in my life was going to fall into place accordingly. I was trusting that I would do my best in all of my efforts. Work. Reading. School. Business. Being there for people. Love. Family. Go down the list, and I was all in. I wasn't interested in killing myself anymore, or whining and complaining about how things were not going my way. I stopped bitching that people were not doing things the way I thought they should be doing them. My energy was flowing endlessly throughout my body and in harmony with the law of the universe. I was manifesting my desires, my feelings, my relationships, my life. The grass was always greener, the sky a brighter blue, the lights were shinier, the flowers smelled delicious, the air quality was always fresh! This is life!

Think of it like thisWould you make a lunatic move to cross over the highway as oncoming cars come speeding in each direction? No. You'd go under the freeway or find another way around. You would have surrendered to what is. Would you jump off a bridge without a bungee cord? No, because you would fall to your death. You would have surrendered to the laws of gravity. That law will never change. Would you go underwater for longer than you could hold your breath? Again, no. That is, unless you took a deep-sea air tank to assist your breathing. We surrender to survive, so we can see another beautiful day. We all surrender to things every day, despite not putting much thought into it. If we did, we wouldn't have such a fight with life. We give in because we are powerless and lose control over these things. They define a power much greater than we are as human beings. The game of tug of war: Do you remember that game as a kid? One side had to lose. You don't have to lose in life. It's your turn to win!

I was open-minded and wanted to allow everything and anything in. I was out to discover what I had been missing all of this time in life. Bringing in new experiences was not a threat anymore but an opportunity to grow. The same walls that had been keeping out the bad were the walls keeping out the good. I was not afraid to try all life's greatest mysteries. I was going into the unknown, taking a leap of faith, trusting the universe would supply the net. Give it all you've got, I told myself, totally release yourself and live the life you have always wanted. Here are a few tricks I used for embracing my surrender.

- Step up and ask for help. You'll be glad you did.

- Try something completely new and out of this world. Adventure is compatible with growth.

- See things differently. Change the lens on your outdated glasses.

- Let loose. Have fun.

- Have faith. Not doubt.

- Trust your inner self. You are in harmony with the universe.

- Give, love, and empower. There is a purpose.

Chapter 9
Desire to Inspire

"The starting point of all achievement is desire."

—*Napoleon Hill*

There was a young man, you know,

who wanted to make a lot of money

and so he went to this guru, right.

And he told the guru, you know,

I wanna be on the same level

you are and so the guru said

if you wanna be on the same level I'm on,

I'll meet you tomorrow at the beach at 4 a.m.

he like the beach, I said I wanna make money

I don't want to swim the guru said, if you want to make money, I'll meet you tomorrow—4 a.m.

So the young man got there 4 a.m. he all ready to rock 'n' roll.

Got on a suit should of wore shorts.

The old man grabs his hand and said:

How bad do you wanna be successful?

He said: "Real bad."

He said: Walk on out in the water.

So he walks out into the water. Watch this.

When he walks out to the water

he goes waist deep and goes like this guy crazy.

Hey I wanna make money and he got me out here swimming.

I didn't ask to be a lifeguard.

I wanna make money he got me in

so he said come on a little further

walked out a little further

then he had it right around this area

the shoulder area

so this old man crazy

he making money but he crazy.

So he said come on out a little further

came out a little further, it was right at his mouth

my man, I'm about to go back in this guy is out of his mind. And the old man said:

"I thought you said you wanted to be successful?"

He said: "I do."

He said: "Then walk a little further."

He came, dropped his head in, held him down,

hold him down, my man (kept scratching) hold him down,

he had him held down,

just before my man was about to pass out,

he raised him up.

He said: "I got a question for you."

He said: When you were underwater what did you want to do?

He said: I wanted to breathe

He told the guy: He said: *"When you want to succeed as bad as you wanna breathe than you will be successful."*

This is the first half of Eric Thomas's famous "How Bad Do You Want It" speech on YouTube. It has been viewed millions of times on the Internet, and I strongly suggest that, if you are not familiar with it, you watch it in the next twenty-four hours and listen for yourself. It's approximately fourteen minutes and all mighty!

In my opinion, this is by far the best analogy for *desire*. There is irony in Eric's speech. I grew up with asthma, and I was in the hospital because of it. I know very well what it is like not to have access to enough air, almost losing my life from several asthma attacks before the age of five. I was hooked up on tubes so I could stay alive. But very few of us think of things this way when talking about how badly we want to accomplish our primary objectives, our tallest orders. We merely talk about them casually, as if there is no serious intent actually to act upon them. I had to learn the hard way. Nothing comes purely from wishing. You have to decide what you want and go after it with every ounce of energy you have.

So we get stuck. So what? Just because you haven't yet come to a conclusion on what it is you want out of life, don't let that hold you back. I know from experience. For years, I was dancing around jobs, relationships, emotions, you name it, and I was uncertain. It wasn't until I got sober that I stopped joking around with myself and started to take my life a little more seriously. The clock was ticking. My desire was to inspire, to get better, and improve in all areas of my life. I didn't care what I had to do to get there. I know with 100 percent conviction that I will arrive at my destination.

I became obsessed with wanting to get better. Through my journey, I started to discover things about myself that didn't exist before—I had potential! Anything was possible. Nothing could stop me, but me. I took on the role of student so I could learn as much about the outer world as I was learning about myself. I had a thought one day: "If I could open up three businesses while I was in that old frame of mind, then what are the possibilities in my sobriety?" The more I played with the idea, the more I started to unleash the beast from within. I was feeling the monster beneath the surface breaking free!

I knew I needed to educate myself more. If I didn't know what to do, I looked it up and taught myself via the web. Remember, there were no more excuses. I wasn't interested in approaching my future with the attitude that I was only half committed. No, I was all in.

The day that I decided, against all else, that I was going to write this book, I had to face the ugly truth that I was not a writer. Hell, I never even finished a two-page paper in college, and now I want to write a book? "You must be crazy, Manny!" I had so many ideas for writing a book that I juggled for months. I didn't know where to start, how to start, or even what to do after I was done writing. But I knew I had something in the name of desire backing me in the process. Even though I didn't have the answers, I was ready to figure them out. When I started to feel the joy in my life, it dawned on me: everyone who wasn't already in this elated state deserves to get here. It is the only way to live. I was no different from anyone else. I still am an ordinary guy. I just decided to go about my life a bit differently. But what a difference an absolute decision can make. Because I was so thrilled to share this feeling with the world, and because I was watching all kinds of experts share their stories, helping the greater population, it was in those defining moments I decided it was time to flip the script. I wanted to write and speak about my journey to help transform lives, to put an end to suffering as I knew it.

Desire is a universal language. An article I read online in a success magazine says, "Desire grips people with an insatiable appetite for action. If you have sufficient desire to succeed, nothing can stop you from becoming a winner, a leader, or a high performer. Desire is the burning internal quality that pushes you and produces a restlessness with things as they are. Desire empowers you to meet the challenges of life and compels you to fulfill a purpose larger than yourself."

When you make a definite decision to back all of your desire, you better get ready to burst through all of the barriers holding you back. Are you ready? You turn into a superhuman, you feel it, you express it, and the world you want is now yours. Nothing can stop you. You might have villain after villain come at you but, just like the Hulk, all you do is knock them away and keep moving forward on your desires. You're powerful! You must remember that it will get hard and you will be at risk but, without a definite decision, you would stop trying and quit. Uncomfortable is part of the challenge, and the goal is to embrace the uncomfortable. If everyone could handle being uncomfortable, then everyone would be living the life they always dream of. Look around and observe that one; nature doesn't lie.

Let's take a look at some circumstances where, against all odds, a few of the world's most successful individuals never gave up.

Michael Jordan: Cut from his high school basketball team, he kept going and said, "I've missed more than 9,000 shots in my career. I have lost almost 300 games. 26 times, I've been trusted to take the game-winning shot and missed. I've failed over and over and over again in my life. And that is why I succeed." As said in Nike Culture: The Sign of the Swoosh.

J. K. Rowling: Rowling was broke, depressed, and trying to raise a child on her own while attending school and writing a novel. She went from depending on welfare to survive to being one of the richest women in the world in a span of only five years through her hard work and determination.

Oprah Winfrey: Oprah faced a hard road to get her celebrity status, enduring a rough and abusive childhood as well as numerous career setbacks, including being fired from her job as a television reporter because she was "unfit for TV."

Walt Disney: Disney was fired by a newspaper editor because he lacked imagination and had no good ideas. After that, he started a number of businesses that didn't last too long and ended with bankruptcy. He kept plugging along, however, and eventually found a recipe for success.

These stories are happening every day. Once you reach a decision to work on your goals, are you going to do everything it takes to get what you want?

Are you going to choose to write your book over watching Breaking Bad?

Are you going to choose reading a book over chasing Pokémon?

Are you going to cut out all distractions?

I know that entertainment is what drives us nowadays, but how many of you will be driven by achievement? You have one life. Give it everything you have!

Every morning when I wake up and every night before I go to bed I visualize what I want in my life. I use a vision board. It's hanging right next to my desk. I'm glancing at it as I sit writing this book. It is a constant reminder that I have a dream, and if something fails, to adjust the plan, and go after it with plan B. Be tenacious. Be so hungry that you stay up for days working toward your dream. This is a dream, and I am living my dream. Wow!

You don't have to be a genius to make your dreams come true, so get past that mental block. The Wright Brothers were two bicycle mechanics who created the airline industry as we know it today. Bicycle mechanics! Sir Edmund Hillary and Tenzing Norgay were the first people to climb Mt. Everest, doing it with no idea how it was going to be done. They just knew that they were going to do it. And they did. Out of desire. Many people perished up on that mountain, attempting to hit the summit. Once they reached the top, thousands of people followed. Because they knew that it was now possible. If it has been done, then why can't you do it?

The greatest truth is that when you want something badly enough, you'll do anything to get it, and get it you will. Think about all of the small successes you've had in a lifetime. You are already successful! Now it's time to take it up a notch, even if you think it's too outstretched of a goal. And let me tell you, if you know how to reach your goal, you're not dreaming big enough.

Once I understood how important desire was, I was intent on creating a system that would never allow me to fall back. I knew there would be tough days, but I wanted to know *why*, when I had a rough day, I would get up and follow the routine as planned. I wanted to know *why*, when I felt like having a drink, I would say no. I wanted to know *why* I was out to create the life I had always envisioned. So I asked myself over and over again, and my *why* was revealed.

- **For my mom.** My mom went to hell and back one too many times, fought the odds, and worked too hard for me not to be great. I want to make her proud and continue her life's work, to leave a legacy on her behalf. Inspiring and helping people alleviates the suffering in their lives.

– **For my dad.** He was a single father and did everything he could to make me the man I am today. I want to make him proud. I don't want to be the broken, worthless man I was for years, full of empty promises and failed attempts. I don't want him to have to worry about retirement. I don't want him to have to worry about money. I want him to be able to enjoy his life. I want him to flourish in his hobbies and live the way he never got to, because he blessed me in so many ways.

– **For freedom.** To travel, to come and go as I please, to explore and adventure with no strings attached. To be at peace all the time, going with the flow of the universe.

– **For control.** I get to make my own decisions, damn it. That is that!

Think of the reasons that will *turn you on* as I mentioned just above. These reasons are powerful, and they can serve as never-ending motivation on the dark days.

These are three reasons for doing well and pushing people to their limits.

- Personal reasons:
  - Recognition
  - Respect

- Feeling

- The desire to win

- Joy, satisfaction, pleasure

- Family reasons: STRONG!

  - Some people do well for others

  - Humans are greatly affected by others

- Hard little reasons

  - Budget

  - Finance

  - Promotion

  - Advancement

Find your sweet spot in these categories. Ask yourself, "Why am I after what I desire." Remember, there are many people out there living their dream, and now it's your turn to live yours. You are capable of being on top of the world. Find your passion and tap into the potential you have. Turn up the dial on your desire, and watch the joy rise.

Chapter 10
Learn More to Earn More

"Learning is the only thing the mind never exhausts, never fears, and never regrets."

—*Leonardo Da Vinci*

Do you remember when you were a kid, and why you asked so many questions:

Why is the car red?

Why does the dog bark?

Are we there yet?

Why is the sky blue?

Where do babies come from?

It's because as kids we were innately *inquisitive*. We were natural wonderers of the world around us. We had a desire to learn unconsciously. Point blank, kids just want to better understand everything their senses are picking up in their environment. Kids are not purposely trying to drive their parents off the wall but, for some parents, the pounding pressure of question after question, might drive them to pop their tops off. So in most cases, mom and dad begin to tell their children to stop asking so many questions and, as a result, they curb the young child's curious nature and desire for more knowledge. This action that can really hurt long-term learning and development.

They grow up with this idea in the back of their minds: "Mom and Dad always told me to stop asking questions, so I guess I'll sit here in the corner and, when I am curious, I'll just keep my mouth shut." Please do not let this be you, parents or children. Being on a constant, never-ending pursuit for answers through asking questions is fundamental for success, happiness, and fulfillment. We must relentlessly search for knowing the basics: Who? What? When? Where? Why? How?

You should always be asking questions in class, at work, and over the phone with friends, in anything you do. Questions are what provide us with new insights, answers we are looking for, and additional wisdom. Questions open up new doors and keep the muscles of the mind hard at work.

One of the greatest tragedies on this planet is that we stop learning. But we are never too old or too young to learn more. With the amount of information circulating in the world today, we should never sleep unless we need the rest. There is always something to learn, gain, and improve upon. It is an attitude. As Benjamin Barber said, "I don't divide the world into the weak or the strong, or the successes and the failures…I divide the world into the learners and the nonlearners."

I was a nonlearner for years. I gave up on education at an early age. In fact, during high school, I remember the curriculum being a walk in the park. There were no challenging ideas or thoughts. Or maybe there were, and I just found a way to cheat through them. I was often bored in geometry class with my head on the desk, drool forming a pool close to my mouth. "Manny, if you keep falling asleep, I will kick you out of my class," would say my teacher. "Ah, this stuff is so irrelevant to life, why should I pay attention?" I would think. Year after year, I was keeping up with my studies, but I was far from maintaining a desire to keep learning in the future. I remember thinking on many occasions, "I can't wait for school to be over." I never read the class materials. I would just browse the books, skimming over the main chapters, and hoping that I connected to the right idea present on the next exam. When it came time for tests, I would sit next to the smarter students and try to cheat off of them. I am talking about years of this same behavior. And I got away with it every time. It certainly showed, though, as I went away to college and was introduced to the idea of studying.

In college, you are preparing for the real world. A career, a business, whichever route you please. That is, unless you were me. I went to a very high academic school in San Francisco, and fell behind the first semester. I am convinced now that the one and only thing that kept me in school was baseball. Had it not been for athletics, I may have dropped out sooner. But I was under the pressure to be all that I could be in sports, while some of my family members were excelling at their studies.

I didn't want to be a moron and show up as the loser. When the homework was assigned, though, I was no longer able to copy off of everyone else, which means I had to set aside time from entertainment to get work done. This was a foreign concept to me. This wasn't the system I was used to back home, during high school. If I didn't get my shit together, it was going to be a huge waste of $40,000 for an academic year worth of tuition, money my dad definitely did not have to throw away. I paid close attention to all of my peers. They were focused, and they got it. "I am here to get my studies done and earn a degree," was spilling from their thoughts. Today, I say this truthfully: The only regret I have in life is not graduating from the University of San Francisco, where I was so graciously accepted to extend my learning career.

Once I was an official dropout from college, I cut off all opportunity for learning. I was stubborn and thought I had accumulated all of the knowledge possibly available. Boy, was I wrong. I often laughed and wondered why people would go back to school at such a later age, an idea I was completely opposed to for the longest time. My family always encouraged me to get back into school during my twenties. And I always said, "Never. I can't find any value in learning anything else from school. It has nothing to do with what I want to do now."

Most of us turn off the learning switch after graduating from college. Many do graduate, of course, and I support everyone who has taken the time to get a degree. The traditional education timeline closes up in one's twenties. We start to get involved in other attention-grabbing activities: entertainment, TV, movies, happy hours, Twitter, Xbox. None of these are true learning tools, and they take up our most precious asset, time. If you have a job, then you might be thrown a workshop bone here and there; but chances are, after on- boarding and orientation, the learning curve takes a steep dive. Only then are you required to take the occasional systems update and policies test. If you are higher in the food chain, then you will undoubtedly be required to maintain competency for that specific technical skill. But what about yourself? What about the higher education of you? Wouldn't you like to know more about your abilities? What you are capable of? How great you can be? What your feelings are?

To my disappointment, there is no formal education here. No one teaches this material in any school—not in undergraduate or graduate programs…or anywhere. When people are caught up in "the battle of the bigger degrees" conversation (i.e., "I am better than you are because I have a master's degree and you only have a bachelor's degree"), it is comical. In modern society, we are judged by how many years of school we complete. Many of the world's most successful individuals, including those who have changed the course of history, were high school and college dropouts. I believe the highest level of education is the understanding of you:

- Loving yourself
- Knowing why
- Knowing your purpose
- Knowing your feelings
- Being consciously aware of your environment
- Being open to all possibilities
- Understanding self-management
- Being involved in relationship management
- Growing every single day

This is a joyous feeling, and the best degree to earn is the one that has your stamp on it. It's a customization of yourself. Unfortunately, today, no prospective employer asks about your self-education, an education that separates the educated person from the uneducated person. Or the learner from the nonlearner.

Take into consideration the following words from Napoleon Hill, from his ever-popular book Think and Grow Rich. "Many people make the mistake of assuming that, because Henry Ford had but little 'schooling,' he was not a man of 'education.' Those who make this mistake do not understand the real meaning of the word educate. That word is derived from the Latin word 'educo,' meaning to educe, to draw out, to develop from within. An educated man is not, necessarily, one who has an abundance of general or specialized knowledge. An educated man is one who has developed the faculties of his mind that he may acquire anything he wants, or its equivalent, without violating the rights of others."

So, here I was confronted with the scary truth that I needed to become a student again. I was approaching age thirty, and I needed some change. Once I realized that my journey wouldn't continue the way I imagined if I didn't take the time to learn more about myself, the world around me, and other people, then I was screwed. I was committed to investing in myself continuously. I was excited by looking over my prospects of constant, never-ending improvement in the areas that mattered. I bought one book, read it, and then bought another. I finished that one, and then bought two more, and finished them. I had only read eight books in thirty years before this time, and I mean that. And with those books, I didn't retain the knowledge because I wasn't fully present in my reading. My mind was elsewhere. Now, I was at eight books in two months. I had a new desire and a new discipline. I was drawing from within, reading books on happiness, love, giving, and mindset. Each book gave me some new insight into the beauty, the essence, the surprises, and the adventure that life has to offer. Being a book nerd never felt so good. I would get excited to pass on a nice dinner and come home to read. I knew that my return on investment was under my control in these circumstances. I proudly say that, as I write this chapter, I have completed the reading of fifteen books in a few months. The average adult reads one book per year.

I also enrolled in several continuing-education classes, and sat in on college classes at the local university to check in and pick up some extra knowledge (only in areas that I was interested in). I spent my money on traveling to various cities and attending seminars and workshops. What a treat it is to meet with likeminded people and build relationships. I hired a coach for my speaking and voice. She has become one of my dearest friends, and she beats my ass into a pulp when we work together. But I grow! I am better at the end of the session.

I encourage you to find someone who has done the job you are looking to do or built the business you want to build. He or she will know the system and the process and can help you. Don't be afraid to show up at a professional's front door and ask for help. These people leave clues for you to be successful, and the first thing they want is to be able to share their valuable insight with someone who's all in for learning. Become so resourceful that nothing can stop you in your studies. Use all available information to help you become better. Like Jim Rohn says, "Don't wish it was easier, wish you were better. Don't wish for less problems, wish for more skills. Don't wish for less challenge, wish for more wisdom."

Get over the idea that you know everything already. Because I hate to break it to you, you don't! I thought I did, and I had a one-way ticket to nowhere. The greatest minds on earth commit to learning one thing, based on their area of interest. Try not to waste your time learning about things that aren't relative to your interest. Time is our greatest resource. Be wise with it. You can be just OK at several different jobs, or you can be great at one. You make the choice and choose wisely. And remember, find your inner kid if you are curious and, for god's sake, just *ask the question.*

Learn more to earn more is not just about making more money. It is about developing, from the inside out, all of the areas in your life that matter—health, wealth, love, happiness to become the best you. You might think you know everything there is to know about you. If you are content, great! But I assure you, only the tip of the iceberg is noticeable. You are a special human being and have a story to share with the world. Go out and inspire people, influence them to make a difference, get them to take action on being a student again, and explain to them the benefits of discovering one's true self. You'll be glad you did.

PART THREE:
THE REFLECTION

Chapter 11
Forgiveness for Freedom

"Forgiveness is the final form of love"

—Reinhold Niebuhr

The date is February 7 and it's Super Bowl Sunday. I am geeked up, my way of saying I'm so excited to watch the one NFL team I adore, the Denver Broncos, take another stab at winning the championship. "But you're from Las Vegas," you might ask, "How are the Broncos your favorite team?" Good question. Here is the answer. As I kid, I chose three teams to follow and stick with throughout my life. It is that simple. For baseball, I would always watch the Atlanta Braves on TBS. It was between the Braves and the Cubs, because both played on national TV. But the Braves were the more winning team, and I liked winners. For the NBA, it was the Lakers. Their games were on FSN, and I would catch a glimpse from time to time while I was flipping through the channels; plus the city itself was close and still is one of my favorite places to visit. I know, it was an odd way of choosing, but hey, it is what it is. And then there were the Broncos. I was drawn to Terrell Davis and John Elway. After making the decision, I kept my word and stayed a Broncos fan, even through the rough years.

The team was left with disappointment after disappointment for years, but I still had a lot of faith, and the third whack at a championship was sure to be the charm in Peyton Manning's Denver playoff career. After all, the guy is a class act and deserves to win, right? I think everyone was rooting for him, purely out of respect. The Vegas casinos were very heavy with betting activity, even though the numbers weren't looking good for Denver as a favorite. Sports fans were throwing down on a Carolina win over Denver. "No," I said to myself. "I can't watch them lose again!"

Meanwhile, it was 2:03 p.m., one hour and twenty-seven minutes before game time, and I had just sent the following text message to my aunt Danielle in Miami. I should have called, but I was scared…the facts I needed were going to cause a seismic shift in my life.

"Hi there! I wanted to see if you were free at some point this week to ask you some questions about my mom and understand a lot more of what she was like and what you two went through. I am going through a magical self-discovery process, and I need to know what exists at the core of me by tracing it back in time. This is something I should have done a long time ago. If you are available, it would be great to talk!" I followed it with a smiley-face emoticon.

Her response came one hour and nine minutes later, at 3:12 p.m.

"Hello! I'm sitting here with tears in my eyes as I'm reading your text. I knew this day would come, and I am more than happy to share your mom's story with you. I don't want to do it on the phone. I'll come to Vegas, and we will sit down and do it face to face. I hope you are ready for it. I think of you often, and I'm so disappointed in myself for not keeping in touch with you. I get your news from Nathaniel, so I think that's one of the reasons I don't make more of an effort. I'm not on Facebook either, and that's how everyone stays connected...I love you very much and am so grateful you're in my life and that my children have a relationship with you. I'll let you know when I'm coming, it will be sometime this month. Love, Danielle"

So why is this important?

Let me take you back in time twenty years...

I was ten years old, sitting in the house that I grew up in on Duke Johnson, when the phone rung, a phone call that would change my life. I answered and said "Hello." My very young kid's voice was receiving the call. On the other end I heard, "This is the San Bernardino County Coroner's Office. Can I please speak with Manuel?" Manuel is my father's name. He was known for a long time as big Manny, while I was little Manny, until I grew up physically and now stand several inches taller than him. In this moment, though,

I had a bad feeling. I knew something was wrong. They asked for "Manuel."

A few days later, I was playing outside my dad's girlfriend's house, running around like ten-year-old kids do. I remember watching my dad come out of the front door and head my direction. I thought I was in trouble. I sensed something was up, but I was unsure of what the trouble was. Regardless, something was wrong, and I could smell it. "Manny, come over here please." Just as soon as I got into his circle, the energy was gone. He started to speak, and I watched a waterfall of tears come cascading down his face. My dad is tough, so I'm thinking to myself, what could possibly have him in tears right now? And the words that followed brought it all together. Although I was young, I understood very clearly what came out of his mouth. "Son, I don't know how to tell you this, but your mother has passed away…" He reached over to hug me, and hold me tight in his arms…

"What do you mean, dad?"

"She's dead, son…she is not coming back"…Then sobs.

"What happened to her, dad?"

"They told me that she was very sick and needed to go to a better place…" Sobs.

How do you process this as a little kid? Did I know what this really meant?

As it turns out, my mother had ovarian cancer and passed away at a very young age. She was thirty-two years old.

For days upon days, I remember lying around sobbing, thinking, wondering why me, why my mom? I barely had enough quality time with her to reference my memory to cherish the good times we had together. But the truth was that she rarely found her way into my life from the age of five until her passing. The only resource I had was now depleted, *hope*. I hoped that one day my mother would come back and be an active participant in my life. I wanted my mother to be there for me. Not for someone else's life. Just mine. And until that heartbreaking day, I always believed that maybe, just maybe, she would come around one more time to hug me, kiss me, and love me. However, with this heartbreaking news, all hope was lost.

I was mad, selfish, guarded, and resentful for twenty years about my mother's passing. How could she do this to me? I didn't want to know the truth about the details. Quite honestly, I didn't give a shit about knowing before I decided to stop drinking and partying, because I was too busy hiding the pain behind all the distractions. But it was now time to find out more about the life that my mom lived, so that I could find out more about myself. Why did I behave the way I did? Was it because of some genetic congruency? I was her son, and I couldn't link anything until I surrendered to the fear of being vulnerable and realized it was OK to meet my mom, at least what I could of her. I wasn't going to be surprised if my mom was an alcoholic, drug addict, and emotionally abused in her upbringing. I was ready for it all. Tell me everything. Just give it to me. Here I am, open ears and open mind.

My aunt arrived in Las Vegas nine days after I texted her that Super Bowl Sunday. She was going to be staying for a week. I knew this was going to be an emotional ride. Although I was scared, I was excited too, because I knew that once I confronted the truth, all the pressure of anguish would fade away, two decades worth of it.

I wasn't interested in wasting any time. I wanted to get right to the meat. I had pen and paper, my voice recorder, tissue, and courage ready to listen. I had so many questions. What was my mom's life like? How was she as a person? What did she deal with before she died? Where did she come from? Did she drink? Did she do drugs? How were her relationships? How did she treat me even when she was troubled?

Here is what I found out, as Danielle tells me:

"Your father got a hold of me and told me that they had found her and that she was dying…She was in a hospice in California. I was trying to get in touch with her and I never could. I tried so hard to find her. I talked to your mother as she was dying in the hospice over the phone, and *Her last requests from me were pajamas and candy. She loved candy…it was just before they took her off of the morphine…She didn't have anything...Nobody was there with her...She died alone."*

My aunt tearfully explains, and by now I am shedding my own, that "she sounded like a happy teenager again. I prepared the box with those last requests and sent it to her, only to have it returned with big letters, "DECEASED," written on the box in the return mail.

My mother did everything she could, physically and emotionally, to love me, and give me all of her resources—not physical resources, but emotional resources. The effort was there, and that mattered indefinitely. All of what she was capable of, she gave. She didn't have the right tools to be effective in keeping herself under control. Her childhood was abusive. Her mother never trusted her. She was always the one being blamed. She was a drug addict. She was an alcoholic. Her family was picking up and moving every month. Never was there any stability. My grandmother, my mom's mom, was always dating and bringing new men into the picture. Grandma was also a big drinker, and she didn't have many life skills to pass down to my mother, or to my aunt, only the survival skills. *Mom you are amazing and I love you so much!*

My father and I never talked about my mom. I knew he was reserved in discussing her death and his feelings, which was a bad habit I picked up from him. I know he was damaged because of her death, too. It was a matter of being tough. Because that's what grown men do. And they want their kids to be strong, which I totally understand; but being tough only got me a one-way ticket to living the most insecure life. I do know that, through the words of my aunt, my father absolutely loved my mother to death, and he would have done anything to see to her survive and heal. This breaks my heart, because I always knew my dad was a man of love. I don't remember their marriage; I was too young. While my aunt often spoke highly of him, I have never seen him since behave in that loving way. But his intentions were very equal to my mother's when it came to raising me.

The reflection and confrontation with the truth was magical. Once I found out how wonderful of a woman my mom was, despite all her troubles, I knew I had those same qualities inside of me. I was blessed to have been passed along such characteristics from her. She left an impact on my life and is very much still a part of my life, sitting right at the core of my pumping heart. I was the pride and joy of my parents' lives.

I cried the next day when I woke up and read from my journal, from the category "What I am grateful for in my life." I read from it daily, and it reminded me how fortunate I was. The day after my aunt helped repair my heart, I broke into tears after reading the first line: "I am so grateful for the love of my family!"

Here I was, truly appreciating that, even though my mother had been gone for 90 percent of my life, I knew, genuinely knew, that I was encapsulated in balls of love. I was complete and love was pouring in. For the first time, I was in a state of forgiveness. Forgiveness was the new path to my freedom. I was on this journey to find out more about myself but, when I learned about my mother, I was all-powerful and capable. I am here now, and I am going to conquer my world. I want to make both my mom and my dad very proud. I owe it to them. They did all they could to the best of their ability to raise me, right or wrong, and it's not about the outcome. It's about the effort. And I applaud them. I love them both very much!

During this momentous week, my aunt said to me, "I am stepping in, and taking the role of your mother." I gracefully accepted, as a new a child of love. I could feel it, give it, and accept it. Save yourself the inward misery, and just accept that what is done is done. You don't deserve to suffer and, remember, it takes subjection and courage to forgive and to walk down memory lane…Land of the *free*.

Chapter 12
Gratitude, My New Attitude

"Gratitude turns what we have into enough, and more. It turns denial into acceptance, chaos into order, confusion into clarity...it makes sense of our past, brings peace for today, and creates a vision for tomorrow."

—*Melody Beattie*

Here in the US of A, we traditionally identify the start of the holidays as Thanksgiving Day, an annual celebration for the blessings of the past year that occurs on the fourth Thursday of every November. For many families, the preparation often starts weeks before the big day arrives and, as it approaches, it causes everyone involved in planning to stress. Planes, trains, and automobiles are revving their engines. The kids, away at university, are booking flights for a cross-country journey to the homeland. Mom and dad foot the bill because, god knows, most college kids are broke. Cousins are loading up their cars and plunging the oil to make the four-hour drive from Southern California to Nevada.

Meanwhile, back in the old nest egg, grandma takes cooking matters into her own hands and prepares a very traditional combination of hers. Rice and beans we all love of course, among other things, but who says rice and beans don't go well with turkey, cranberry, and yams? Aunts and uncles are in town, busy getting their own meals planned for their respective spouse's family. Two Thanksgivings! Mmmm. The conversations about thankfulness are at an all-time high. However, for me, during this most precious time, the conversations were lame. The day was just another reason to eat a lot of well-cooked savory food that I took no part in helping make. So, more or less, it was another food and football day. Ugh...the Cowboys and Lions. At least I'll be somewhat entertained.

"Manny, are you coming to join us for Thanksgiving?" asks my grandma days before.

"Yes, I'll be there..."

"OK. We'll see you Thursday, then." End conversation.

But wait a second...

Shouldn't I be excited about getting to spend time with Aunt Lucy, Cousin Andrea, and Uncle Gabe, Grandma? Shouldn't I be more involved in preparing the cranberry, the ham and turkey, and the homemade fruit salad? Or am I the grandson, the son, the cousin, the nephew, that just shows up with his hands out, ready to eat his two full plates when they are put on the table and served to him? Gimme gimme gimme.

I hadn't been involved in the joyful process of appreciation until now. I had been more concerned with how shitty it was that I had to work that night, when I should have been grateful that I had a job. How I was jealous of friends, because they had deeper relationships with their families, and more connected in love than I was, when I should have been grateful I had a family. I distanced myself as far as I could from feeling the love; it was my wrongdoing. The meaning I applied to the Thanksgiving holiday and to life was take-take-take…and then everything was taken from me. I would always think, what can I take from this? I was an ungrateful SOB. I am not surprised I endured all the misfortune and loss over the years.

I was in a terrible state of gratitude for as far back as I could remember. Not because I wasn't taught the right way; in fact I was. But I chose to be the punk I was because it was a numbing mechanism. I wanted to be the victim, the one everyone felt sorry for. Plain and simple, I just expected to receive without giving. Hands open, fingers motioning back in my direction. Even though I would say *thank you*, did I really understand the larger picture of thanks? I should have been chomping at the bit to share precious time with my family. It would have been the perfect time, year after year after year, to stand with Grandma and ask her questions about the dishes she prepared. It was a perfect time to talk with my uncle about his golf game and genuinely care about his progress, or even sit with my cousin Teri, who I was lucky to get a word in with when she walked in the door (only to have no further conversation with her over the course of the night). At most, it was "Hey, how have you been?" Umm, that's not sufficient Manny. I was underestimating the value of the abundance I had in my life right in front of me. Every single day, there is an opportunity to express thanks. Just make the phone call, write and send the letter, tell your dad you love him. It's easy, but I was always thinking about what I didn't have, and that robbed me of my soul and my spirit.

Gratitude is a state of being...or not being, if you aren't aware. And we are human *beings*, so live gracefully!

Thanksgiving is about human connection. After all, isn't all of life supposed to be that way? Why did we get pushed into the idea that thankfulness is only appropriate to express on Thanksgiving? What about the other 364 days of the year? For those of you who walk around with your head high in appreciation, the world needs more of you. Teach your peers to be the same. And, in time, the world will become more lovable. I assure you, the ones who have mastered the skill of grace live the most fulfilled lives, every day.

When I decided to reflect deep into the ugly years of my life, I was able to identify all the points of selfishness that got me through so many holidays and the remaining calendar days as well, very unhealthily.

Let's take a peek at some lame stories that were apparent in my life.

BUSY ME

I was too busy with partying and chasing chicks. This got in the way of my everyday chance to be more appreciative. I was once again working from habit. We are so naturally overwhelmed with phones, TV, work, meetings, kids, girlfriends, boyfriends, and aimless wandering, that it's easy to overlook, and set aside a time each day and night, to take some time for yourself and think about how wonderful your life really is. Guilty here.

CRUISE CONTROL

I was becoming lazy in my efforts. Life was just drifting, like a directionless boat in the middle of the ocean. I was suffering, but dealing with it every day made me believe this way of approaching my life was OK. Not so true. I was living in my box house, driving to work in my box car, taking the box elevator up the tower, sitting at a box desk...everything was a box in my world. Sure, I just went along with it. What I should have been doing was stepping out into nature, watching the trees grow leaves, taking a swim in the local manmade lake that was constructed decades ago, watching the moon fall behind the clouds just before the rain comes pouring down. This is life, and it was designed to be understood, and not simply walked on. We are creatures of the earth. Do you have any idea how truly blessed we are to live in a land of prosperity?

FAILURE AND RESPONSIBILITY

The mountain of my tragedy and loss was tall. I had failed several times. I was in a poor mental state and, as a result, I didn't look at what I did have to break me out of my funk. Gratitude is an emotion. If it is not used appropriately, then brace yourself for less than the average amount of feel-good moments. I was blaming other people, places, and things. I was always engaged in the complainer conversation, either listening to or telling my victimized story.

Yeah. Yeah..no, this was the real deal. I had to shake things up or my happiness was going to be interfered with. I wasn't willing to accept that anymore. OK. So how did I turn this attitude around and start to welcome more grace into my life? Well, I started with a gratitude journal. And I wrote down everything that I was grateful for in my life.

- the love of my family
- my friendships
- my health
- my job
- my home

- my life

- my freedom

- my faith in myself

- the money I earn

- my ability to serve others

- my ability to make choices

And the list goes on. When you write these down and you read them aloud, it is impossible to live in a suffering state. You can deliberately cultivate an attitude of gratitude by spaced repetition or emotional impact, attaching it to something that moves you by way of the heart. Studies say "gratitude is affiliated with increased energy, optimism, and empathy for others." This is exactly what I was missing from all of my interactions. I created a new discipline. I would now wake up every morning, read off my list, and talk about the things I was grateful for. I do the same thing at night before I go to bed.

It became a pleasure to compliment my family, every last one of them, on something they did well—if they looked good, smelled good, or made a great effort but failed. Done. They had my appreciative support. It was a big step to open up and tell my cousin how much I loved her and that I was thankful for our years growing up. I was setting aside the past. This wasn't just a deliberate change with my family. It was with everyone, every living soul. It was such a good feeling to truly and deeply feel the meaning of thank you when I was using it with the right intentions. This shit sounds so basic, but for me, it was not so easy.

The next step was "OMG" rough. I had to go barreling back in time, where the heartbreak from my relationships left me shattered in a million pieces. I had to confront the harsh truth that I had lost several businesses because of my faults. I had to check in with myself about ruining my baseball career because I was blacking out drunk the night before we were supposed to be on the bus, traveling to a nearby city for a big conference game. The goal was to find the good in all of it and repair the wounds. I felt like I was going to war with myself. I had to stay optimistic and realize that this was good, not painful, no matter how bad it had actually hurt years before.

For example, years ago I went to visit my ex-girlfriend's family in the Midwest for the first time. It was my first time to that part of the country, and it was yet another holiday. This time, it was Christmas. "Manny," she said, "My family gets a bit wild for this Christmas party we have, but it's a lot of fun! We always have a great time." You better believe I was well prepped on "what the family was like" on their home turf for this particular trip. During the car ride in from the airport, her mother was again forewarning me that I would be walking into something I had never seen before. I was just fine and playing it cool. I was more terrified about holding my shit together than anything else.

You know that feeling when you go to stay at your significant other's parents' place for the first time?

"Fuck me, it's nerve-racking, but just behave! Be your best."

"Thank you, ma'am. No sir, I appreciate it, with every sentence!"

"We cook, we dance, we hot tub, we smoke cigars, we make all kinds of wild drinks!" They told me.

"Drinks? Now you're speaking my language!" I was thinking.

I was an unidentified boozing alcoholic! Oh, lord. The family was a great group of people, every one of them very loving. I had a blast until it was time to pack up and come home.

"Ah, Southwest just confirmed our flight was canceled."

"Canceled? How the hell am I going to get home?" I thought with anger.

The snow from the night before blanketed the airport runways. Oh my God. This was the first time I had to deal with the pressure of a canceled flight. I was stressing because Southwest Airlines never lets me down. I had to be at work the next night, and I wasn't going to make it back on time. And I sure didn't want to miss the days because I was missing out on money, and I was still borderline broke.

"I think I am going to stay here a few extra days and spend time with my family," she says to me.

The hell you are woman! I didn't have the balls to say it like that, but sure I was thinking it. But why not stay in her case? Remember that love I mentioned about her way back when; yeah, they figured this part out about life way before I did. This idea I was having no part of.

I said, "You're going to leave me to stay here with them? That's so selfish!"

I had to drive to Wichita, hours away, to catch a flight, through the slick-ass ice in a rental car to make it home on time, and she joined me against her will. My verbal abuse was disturbing; she was hurt. I thought, "OK, I am happy. I got my way. I stayed in control. I am not being chosen over the family." That was something I had to deal with. The envy, jealousy, and fear consumed me. I loved this one, and I didn't want to feel like I was at risk of losing her…to her own family…yuck. I was so reversed in my thinking, but I didn't know any better. As you could imagine, the ride down to the airport and the flight were miserable. We could feel the terrible energy ripping us apart through every calculated mile on the ground and in the air. Why? Because, once again, I was unaware of how to appreciate what I had right in front of me. We ended up fighting for several days after, and I ruined her Christmas, again.

How could I go back into every individual scenario like this one and repair the damage?

I had to go through and take out all of the positives. In that trip, there were 99 percent positives. I'll take those numbers any day. I dropped the resentment, because I looked at the love, the friendships, the smiles, the laughs, nature—hell, I was chopping wood out back with her grandmother. How awesome it was that this woman, in her later years, was chopping wood. Gosh, there is just so damn much to be grateful for in life. And I am thankful for every experience I've had, good or bad, because I know how to apply the right meaning to them now.

Healing requires a trip back in time to breakdown the rough patches and find what good can be preserved. There is much to learn about both yourself and others in the process. We are, as a human race, all the same. Although our experiences are different, we share the same life-form that our family and friends do. We even share the same life-form that complete strangers do. But how beautiful is it that we are all connected to the same energy, and that we can, literally, choose? So, maintain a state of gratitude by taking simple action—the attitude of gratitude starting point.

1. *You can never say enough thanks.* But don't just say it to say it, say it because you mean it! And for god's sake, like Nike says...*Just do it*!

2. *Keep a gratitude journal.* Write down (pen and paper) everything you are grateful for. Read it every day when you wake up and before bed. Do it for one month straight and watch gratitude become your new obsession.

3. *Give your time to help make someone's day!* Find what works best for you. Providing money, joining the local food bank and boxing lunches, or helping autistic kids become better readers are some choices. This will make you cry. By being a part of something greater than yourself, you will feel the ripple of growth and happiness. Life will also return its deepest appreciation for you.

4. *Compliment, compliment, and stop biting your tongue.* I love this one. I once had an overweight guy tell me, "I am having a bad day and I am too ugly" to be up in the club. He had just finished a conference and wanted to feel significant. So I responded to him: "You are ugly compared to who? You are a great looking guy, and it would be our pleasure to have you upstairs in our venue. In fact, I appreciate you for wanting to be a part of our party." He looked and me and said, "Wow, that's the nicest thing that has been said to me today."

Chapter 13
At Your Service

"The best way to find yourself is to lose yourself in the service of others."

—*Ghandi*

Back in 2005, my first ever legal job was on a golf course during my summer break in college. I was on the player services staff at Angel Park. My job duties included cleaning golf clubs, removing trash from the carts and washing them after rounds of golf were finished, and driving customers out to their cars, sparing them a walk. "Thanks, kid, I appreciate the lift, here's five bucks." There were more tasks: driving a range cart in circles to pick up balls (while the young kids aimed for my head in the protective cage), and replenishing the carts with ice, water, tees, and scorecards for the next round of golfers. Later, there was late-night driving around in the carts on the freshly watered hillsides, spinning carts out, and doing donuts like we were in the Indianapolis 500. "Who's closing tonight? Me! All right, let's do a ride around." You bet your ass that was the best part, but it meant a possible delay in getting off work on time. It was an awesome first job!

My idea of service was that one needs to donate countless hours of time, or huge loads of money, to make a difference. But that was wrong, at least for me it was. Early on, I had the opportunity to be of service for nothing but strangers. Eleven years later, I decoded the word service and learned how rewarding being of *service* can be.

For the longest time, I would get upset when people were rude, or they would act as if they thought they were too good to treat others with respect. I wanted them to be much friendlier, but I realized that was a difficult wish without the right toolkit. And returning the rudeness was not being of service to them. So the solution? Be kind, even when they were rude. I thought, "There must be a way to help the people around me to acknowledge that the world is not only about them." Even for me, as torn in life as I was, I always used my kind heart. I wasn't always correct in my behavior, and I know that. But I was so interested in being of service to other people that I forgot to take care of myself. True story. It is important to remind yourself of what kindness is. If you don't have a clue, I've included a definition below.

Kindness is the quality of being friendly, generous, and considerate.

Whenever I would go out for breakfast, lunch, or dinner, in any full-service restaurant where I was being waited on, I always tipped the standard percentage, sometimes over. If I was winning bets, drunk at the blackjack table at 3:00 a.m., you better believe the dealer was getting a nice cut of my earnings. And in the local bars, when I would hit the jackpots, the bartenders always walked away with more than I did, enough to pay their utilities at home. I appreciated the effort of their work because I worked in the same environment over the years. I was very familiar with the nature of the jobs being performed. I cared about making sure they knew I wasn't just another asshole coming into the establishment to be a royal pain in the ass, or out to make the service staff want to run away crying and quit. Trust me, if you work in this business long enough, you'll cross plenty of unhappy patrons. If you are reading this, and you are one of them, lighten up. Respect the people who bust their ass working at restaurants to feed the kids, make the monthly rent, or send money off to grandma because she's sick. They are people just like us, and the job will never be done perfectly. Just be nice for crying out loud!

After permanently returning home from college, I jumped right into the service industry, which in Las Vegas is any restaurant, nightclub, or bar. It was an easy way of saying, yeah, I'm in "that" business whenever anyone would ask. What do you do for work? I got my first restaurant job at the MGM Grand in a fine Italian restaurant called Fiamma. I had no formal experience, but I had the credibility of a college athlete, somewhat, and my prospective boss loved the athlete's mindset, so he gave me a shot. Say it ain't so, but I had to get my hair stripped (to have the drug strain removed so I could pass a drug test) for this job. All of the casino properties did hair tests. I was just starting out, and I was already risking it because I decided to roll a fatty a few months before. Great timing, right? Well, after I got my head burnt and bled out of all the dark color, I was a pure blonde...only for an hour or so. Anyway, I passed and got the job.

I got the job with my then-best friend. We did everything together, including applying for all of the same jobs. It was like a package deal. I laugh about it now but, over the years, we actually were hired to work at five venues together: Fiamma, Striphouse Steakhouse, Boa Steakhouse, XS, and Tryst nightclubs. He and I even did the player services job together on the golf course. Manny and Burt, that's how we were known.

It made this entry-level busser position at Fiamma a lot less threatening. I was comfortable in knowing I had my best friend there close with me, because I was honestly worried I would fuck up. This place was a well-oiled machine, and they were pumping one thousand covers on a concert night, with high-volume and high-check averages. "What the fuck is a cover and a check average?" I remember thinking during my first days working. Do you have any idea how intimidating one's first restaurant job is? It will scare your boots off!

I had no idea how to hold ten glasses in between my fingers, stacks plates on top, while also balancing silverware. This was nuts! I felt so delicate. One wrong turn, and I've just stopped the whole restaurant, midbite, as everyone looks to see who was the sloppy one dropping the table bomb. "Ooooo ahhh" echoes across the room. Managers calmly walk by you with a death stare. I know they were cussing me out on the inside. I could see it in their eyes. But with practice, I got better, and over time, I grew. And after a few years, I was very experienced.

I spent the next eight years in and out of service joints like this one, working for the finest restaurants, bars, and nightclubs in the country. The staff's attitudes were always the same. Las Vegas, Beverly Hills, San Francisco, it didn't matter where I went...it was universal. The menus and the designs of the venues were different, but they were staffed with ordinary people just like me, trying to make ends meet and spieling the house's specials for the night, or educating the customer on the best merlot, from Napa Valley, to buffer their tips. Bussers and waiters, are often scrambling around the restaurant looking for place settings, napkins, and glassware, because the boss is screaming.

"I need a ten top at table two seventy-five, yesterday!"

"Fuck! Yesterday? I wasn't here yesterday." And then I learned that means, now!

"Shit! There are no more plates, silverware is in the wash, and glasses are out!"

So you wait in the dish area for the freshly washed cutlery and glasses, thinking to yourself, "This is it, I'm fired tonight. He asked me one minute ago, but it feels like an hour at this point." Stressful!

Relax, calm down, get in your zone, and trust that you know what you are doing. Be cool, literally. The more you panic, the more stressed you will become. But how to do this when everyone else around you is running around like chickens with their heads cut off, too? Staff would always let the situation and others control them. I was guilty, too, when, really, I should have always been in complete control, control of myself. If I had just taken a step back and understood, in the moment, "I am here, and I have a chance to make someone's day," then you better believe it, I would have. And I needed to understand that I couldn't totally be there for them if I was stressed about their food being behind, or crying over their screaming at me because Pinot Noir was poured instead of Merlot...It was not always our fault. The chef may have been behind on ticket times because one cook went home sick, or maybe the bartender read the label wrong. It's OK! Lighten the load on yourself. Work hard always, but refuse taking all of the blame. Connect to your power source, and trust the fact that you are doing the best you can. Remember to provide more service than you are being paid for.

I love that we always find a way to acknowledge our heroes, and our armed forces, for defending this country and fighting for our freedom. God bless them. They are truly brave souls. But you also have a right to be acknowledged for your everyday service. You are there for someone. You did a good deed. That is life. And we forget to think of it in this way. Be proud of yourself. You can't be sure the neighbor you are about to reach out to didn't just lose a family member, lose a job, or fail a class that would have got them into Yale. He or she could be upset, frustrated, overexcited, for any number of reasons, and it's your job to simply be of service to the person. Smile, open the door, give directions if asked, provide coffee from Starbucks. *Listen!* Everyone wants to be a part of something bigger than themselves. The meaningful journey is where we find the most joy, and being of service to someone will strike some happiness nerves. The benefits of being there for someone are huge. In fact, it feels so good, you'll want to do it over and over again.

I made donating myself, and my time, part of my everyday habits. I meet people from all walks of life, every day, and they are always looking for an answer to some question in mind.

"Excuse me sir, where is the gift shop?"

"What is your recommendation for a show?"

"How can I find the UBER pickup location?"

Most people point and say "there."…noooo! You asshole, you just ruined your chance to be of service, and it was so simple.

"Well, here, let me help you" is a more realistic strategy, being so singularly focused on providing enough information, taking time away from an opportunity to do other things you should be doing, to make sure they know you are there, 100 percent present, and care about the simple answer people are after. It's so easy, people. Care enough about what other people want, help them get it, and you'll get everything in life you've ever wanted. It is the law. Much of the law is that, if you run a red light and are seen by a cop, you will get a ticket. But because we are so consumed in a life of overwhelm and stress, we forget the simple, rewarding things. Simple gestures eliminate our frustrations, and they take no extra effort or financial commitment.

I watch countless people every day pass on the opportunity to be there for someone, and it blows my mind. They are so intent on scrolling through their Facebook feed that they miss the little old lady walking by with her hands full, struggling to carry heavy bags.

"Hey, dude, get off your phone and help her!" one would hope would be the response.

Or, "Hey, there are pieces of trash right in front of you, on the floor. I watched you look at them and keep walking, but don't worry, I'll get them," because I know the guy walking around all day picking up trash, and he rarely gets any help and he deserves a little break.

Or there's the seventy-year-old man bending over and hurting his back, trying to get the gum wrapper that some punk kid dropped knowing he would just come around and get it. I just saved that man a possible back strain and months of missing work from an injury.

"How about this scenario: "Ugh, the bar is so backed up because the conference just let out and I haven't gotten my order taken yet. Well there are fifty other people also waiting for a drink, too, and three bartenders, adequate staffing. Try not to scream at a bartender because he or she hasn't gotten to you. Instead, say "No problem, I see you are working hard. Doing the best you can." And make sure to tip extra for them working their tails off. This would be much like you working hard at your job. This is real life, and the purpose of life is to give or be of service to someone else. Tony Robbins always says, "the keys to happiness are growing and giving." I like to call it service. Make yourself happy by being a part of the movement.

In all of my service industry days, the nightclub experience might have been both my most exciting and the most derailing job ever. Can you imagine the level of patience you need to have? Drunk-ass men and women screaming at you for shot glasses, all the while their breath smells like an ashtray. Then they follow up by spilling their drink on you, and, oh yeah…it was poured just thirty seconds earlier. Minutes later, the table patrons next to you just barfed into the bucket of ice, and now you need to find security to get them kicked out. They had enough! At the same time, you are being bumped in ten different directions, just going with the flow. And now you are only one hour into your twelve-hour shift!

We didn't even get to the make-it-rain tables or the I-want-to-have-a-champagne-fight tables, where it's an all-out waterfall of sticky Dom Pérignon, waitresses freaking out, and managers walking around in their suits and talking into their radios. It was a zoo of drunk people…but who were we to complain? Who were we to miss our opportunity to be a part of someone's memorable, or not-so-memorable experience, depending on alcohol intake? We made great money, we got to watch the best entertainers in the world, and, for the customers who weren't so wasted, we got to build healthy new friendships with them. In hindsight, these were dream jobs. Where else can one be paid to watch entertainment and socialize along with being involved with some slightly stressful work? Isn't that any job? Well, if you give it the negative connotation, then yes. After all, I signed up for it, and knew exactly what to expect nightly.

So this is striking to me. So many people found a way to bitch and complain about how much money they didn't make, or how some guy just knocked over the entire table full of glasses, mixers, bottles, and personal belongings…but what did you expect? Take the service to new heights. Set aside the frustration. The time will pass, and you'll be off spending your hard-earned cash. You deserve it, but don't be sappy in the process. People from all over the world would come to interview for these Vegas jobs, yet the people who had them were constantly complaining about how rough it was, and only finding the joy when work was calm. The attitude is backward. Your worst nightmare is someone's else's best dream. Stop thinking it's so bad. You have no idea how bad really bad is so seize the moment.

I want to stress the importance of this service idea. It can make a huge difference in the world we live in. And with commitments from people who recognize the easy ways to help, serve, be there for someone every day, then the goal of mine to help the world and the world's people become better will be set in motion. We all work in a service job. Whether you are in hospitality or coaching like me, servicing people from all over the world in technology as a computer programmer, servicing some need for a new application that will make Airbnb more functional, or in the medical field as a nurse, gosh, you are blessed to be able to take care of people every day. Do you ever think about how amazing that is? Embrace it in any field you are in. Your life will become more meaningful. I use my days in the service industry to illustrate the opportunity I missed for a decade. I could have made a huge difference in my life early on, and always made a difference for the next person, over and over. I keep these quotes on the whiteboard next to my desk, and I am looking at them right now as I write this chapter.

"Service to others is the rent you pay for your room here on earth."—Muhammed Ali

"The measure of your life will always be in how you serviced others."—anonymous

"We can all be of service to others, and as a result serve ourselves in a higher way."—anonymous

"Give much more than you expect to receive."

—anonymous

Remember, the journey of life and that to find joy is meaningful. There is no limit to what you can do or to how much you can be of service for someone. Choose to make an impact on someone and his or her life by applying some of the following habits, because it's the right thing to do.

Simple gestures or random acts of kindness:

- open the door for someone

- let someone turn before you at the stop

- pick up the beer bottle on the floor so the janitor doesn't have to

- tell the little old lady how pretty she looks today

- bring dad a card and tell him how awesome he is

- SMILE!

Easy, fun, and contagious—aren't they?

Be so singularly present, so focused on listening and paying attention, not just hearing. No daydreaming about your wildest fantasies, no browsing over the shoulder of the person you are in conversation with. Be there for this person. Make him or her feel like a long-lost relative.

Make someone's day with all of the above, and I mean all of it plus engagement. Get him or her involved, and watch your life mean everything to others, because people know you come bearing gifts.

Chapter 14
I Am Worthy

―――――――――👑―――――――――

"No one can make you feel inferior without your consent."

—*Eleanor Roosevelt*

I like the definition of worthy I found in Merriam-Webster. It says: "Worthy: Having enough good qualities to be considered important, useful, etc."

Well, how many is enough? Can we just have one really good one and be useful to someone? What is my significance to my family if I just have OK qualities? Will that affect my worth? Will I feel valued? Will I be enough?

Before my mom died, she and a friend came to pick me up on one of "mom's days." For the record, I rarely got to spend time with her so this was a special day. We were going to get a puppy, and I was with my mommy! I was five years old so there are not too many experiences I can remember from this time of my life. But this chapter is being written because I can remember this day so clearly, as if everything happened yesterday. We were cruising from my dad's house westward through the city, passing the University of Nevada-Las Vegas and Las Vegas Boulevard, before nearing the land where the Orleans Casino sits today. A puppy is a kid's best dream come true but, unfortunately, on this day my dream wasn't coming true, and it could have been my worst nightmare. As we approached the intersection of Cameron and Tropicana to make a left-hand turn on Cameron, with the animal hospital less than a quarter of a mile away, the last words were "Oh my God!"

Then my life went dark, instantly followed by a steady flow of bright clouds—clouds from the heavens blanketing the back of my eyelids. I had no images passing through, no laughs with my mom, no riding around on a tricycle in the park, no perfect days with all my family around me—just a blank canvas, a clear, free, easy life passing in absence of any understanding why this was happening in this moment. And I was still a child, so maybe there was not enough memory to flip through yet?

"Everyone get back! Everyone get back!" I could hear out of one ear, and in the other ear, cries of, "Oh my God, my son, noooo! Please, nooo," followed by more cries. That was my mother screaming and panicking frantically in the background, praying her only son would not lose his life right here, right now. Guys from the corner auto dealership were maintaining control of the scene. I woke up on the street corner after coming back to consciousness extremely dazed and confused. The guys had white towels that were now red from the fountain of blood spewing forth. They were doing their best to stabilize me. "Come on, kid. Hang in there—you can do it! Come on." A few of them were hoping that I wouldn't die in their arms on this ordinary work day for them. "Manny, noooo, please," went mom's cries, a sendoff for me again back into unconsciousness before I could even recognize an ambulance or emergency personnel.

I was dead, my life had ended at five years old…and then I was back to consciousness again. This time I wasn't on the street anymore, but on a stretcher rolling into the hospital, nurses and doctors on my side rushing to get me to the emergency room for a procedure. Then I went into unconsciousness again. "Rest my son." God was looking down on me this day because I woke up several days later. The reality I was about to face was something only very few people experience and more like something you see in a horror movie.

I woke up in a hospital bed, confused and darkened in my thoughts. "Why am I here? What just happened? This is not my bed at home. This is not the front yard I enjoy playing in. Machines, and needles, and people in gowns were everywhere. "Mom? Dad? Why does one of my eyes see a different color every time I blink it? This is new to me. Did I just turn into a superhero? Is this a dream?"

After all, I did love watching Batman, X-men, and Superman as a young child, but not even close, not this time. Maybe someday I would be a superman, but for today I was in a car crash where some man crushed our vehicle on my side going fifty miles an hour. The glass from the windows sliced my face wide open, starting at the forehead and coming down over my eye, onto my cheek area, and even under my chin.

"How could this happen to me?"

"You're going to be fine, my love," my mom whispered.

"Mommy, I don't like this place."

She couldn't help but cry as she watched her son look back at her with a face of fifty stitches. The doctor said I must have closed my eyes as the cars collided and, because of my reaction, I still can see out of my left eye. I was now scarred for life, though, physically and mentally.

One year later, I was engaged in horseplay in my front yard, still recovering and suffering from my accident. Don't all kids play and test the limits? Sure they do. We had this tall, robust, earthly tree that was ideal for climbing. I enjoyed trying to reach new heights, literally. I must have watched too many Tarzan movies in addition to the superhero films, because I sure thought I was a member of the spider monkey family, in the middle of the Amazon jungle except this was the desert southwest. No jungles around here, and I was still a small fry. I didn't even have any experience in tree climbing, just the natural instincts that I had to go up!

I loved the challenge to get up and sit, fifteen feet high above the ground, and look out over the neighborhood. I was up, and on top of the world. As my dad recalls, he was always on the lookout for me, saying, "Be careful, Manny. You're going to hurt yourself."

"No I won't, Dad, I am good at this! See!"

I did great for a long time until the I-told-you-so day arrived. Sure enough, I was on my vertical climb to the first stepping point, where I would branch off onto other areas of the tree. When my grip slipped, I was in free fall to the unforgiving ground. Ten feet later, I landed on my right wrist. Snap! My wrist broke immediately from the weight of my young body, crushing it with hundreds of pounds of pressure. I looked down at my arm and I was a bit grossed-out. My wrist was curled up under my forearm in the shape of a U. I knew I wasn't this flexible, plus the pain was excruciating. And now, it was time to get in the car and go see the doctor. I was in shock from the damage.

By age six, I was scarred on my face and had tested the laws of gravity, which resulted in a broken right wrist. The physical damages would heal, as the body is designed to do, but how about the emotional scarring? I wasn't prepared to combat the heavy pressure of school, classmates, and family. I was still a growing kid and, now, I had to work harder than most to fit in. My face created a stir with everyone, and I mean everyone. I looked like a monster or some kid who wore a Halloween mask at all times. I was submerged with questions. "Oh my God, what happened? Who did this to you? Can you still see?" And comments like, "You're going to be scarred on your face for life. "That's ugly," some of my classmates would say. They didn't know any better. "Ew, you're lucky you didn't die," was another one, and the list goes on. I would walk into class every day, the kids would laugh hysterically, and point me out, with every ounce of energy they had. I was now becoming the class clown, and it wasn't because I was funny, but clearly I looked funny to everyone else. Here I was taking an enormous amount of ridicule during the developmental phase of my life, when I should have been establishing my identity. Today, twenty-four years later, I am still asked questions about my scar.

I was disturbed, left out, and made fun of for many years to come. I couldn't find a sweet spot for fitting in. After I broke my arm, I had to go back to class in a full arm cast. I had trouble sleeping with this damn thing, and I remember having to sleep on my back with my arm straight up because, if it fell parallel to the bed, I would be in severe pain and the stress on my tiny muscles would be very uncomfortable. I was in first grade at the time and my teacher's name was Ms. Johnson. She was a nice lady, but she couldn't have done anything to help me get over the mental block. She had a full class to work with and, because I was limited in my writing, I was getting frustrated. To be honest, I was giving up already. Oh, man, if only I knew how "giving up young" would affect my future. I wasn't able to keep up with the other students and, naturally, I took on the idea that I wasn't smart enough. Pressures began mounting again from an academic angle. I remember sitting in class, watching all the other students work on their assignments while I was told to just sit there and do what I could.

"Manny, how are you doing over there?"

"I am fine, Ms. Johnson."

I was drawing stick figures, nothing more than the occasional doodle if you will, while the others were making academic progress. At times, I would get so frustrated that I attempted to write with my left hand, but it took me five minutes to dot one I. Next! My future was being shaped in advance, sitting right there in my first-grade classroom, where learning is supposed to be fun, interactive, and growth-minded. For me, it was the beginning of not believing I was worth it, good enough, smart enough, or important enough. This was the real deal, and I had some tough walls to break down in the future if I was ever to get over the trauma.

I found some helpful information to sum up my early years. The impact of the wounds would be felt long after those back-to-back years. Here is some developmental information I read in The Future of Children publication by Jacquelynne S. Eccles.

"From age:

3 to 6 years—Initiative vs. guilt: Children want to undertake many adult-like activities, sometimes overstepping the limits set by parents and feeling guilty.

7 to 11 years—Industry vs. inferiority: Children busily learn to be competent and productive or feel inferior and unable to do anything well.

Each period is marked by basic biological and cognitive changes, as well as changes in the social surroundings where children's daily lives unfold. Exercising their growing autonomy in school and organized programs, children learn about the world outside the family, match themselves against the expectations of others, compare their performance with that of their peers, and develop customary ways of responding to challenges and learning opportunities. Through these years, they forge a personal identity, a self-concept, and an orientation toward achievement that will play a significant role in shaping their success in school, work, and life."

Guess which side of the above statements was relative to me? Both! I was sitting pretty ugly right in the middle.

In the years following my mother's death, I was raised by a single parent, with the help of other family and family friends. The reality was that I was scarred, broken, abandoned, and motherless, all by the age of ten. It wasn't until many years later that I would discover the influence of my uneasy childhood. When my mom passed away, I had just gotten started in Little

League baseball and, recently, I asked my father, "What was it that made me want to get into baseball?"

He laughed and said, "One day were outside in the front yard, you were playing with your ninja turtle action figures. You were throwing them up, watching them tumble through the air and back into your hands. Until one day you didn't snag them. This time the plastic green turtles fell to the concrete floor and shattered!"

"That's it!" He looked and me and said, "Come on. We are going to the store. You won't break anything anymore. I can't keep buying all kind of toys."

He bought me a bat, a glove, and a ball. My obsession didn't take long to materialize. After a few months, he told me to stay on the lookout for the tryout schedule on the bulletin board at my elementary school, so I wasted no time in gluing my eyes to that board every day, hopeful that paper would be posted so I could find out about tryouts. "Dad! Dad! Dad!" I got the paper! Can I play now? Please, please?" And the rest is history.

I had found a new hobby, one that I believe truly saved my life. I had nothing else to work with, but by the grace of God I was talented enough to excel in baseball. And I did excel, competitively, year after year, from age ten through nineteen. This became my life. And by the time I failed to make it past the collegiate rankings, I falsely believed baseball was all I had to survive on. This meant a free-fall plunge into the abyss.

My self-image was destroyed. I was nearly dead twice, ugly, stupid, a cheater, and overweight, with crooked teeth. I was a failure by this point. It's no surprise that I couldn't find the confidence to take action or follow through in my life. I had frustrating limitations squatting in place. A crummy self-image set the boundary, and it was going to affect my individual accomplishments until I repaired it.

I couldn't fulfill my desire for success, because I always trumped that feeling through a belief of unworthiness. I sabotaged my opportunities because I thought, "This won't happen. It will never happen." For some reason, I never felt worthy. The one person who is supposed to intrinsically make me feel wanted, loved, and worthy is my mother, and she was gone now. I continually and cyclically sabotaged my success, and then what success I did have would be pulled out from under me, which is what I used to do. I would think,

"Why would anything go right for me?"

"Why would I come up?"

"I don't ever catch a break."

"I will never get it."

This all came from a defeating self-image. In relationships, I found myself thinking, "I am undeserving because my mother didn't want me, so why would anyone else want me?" My mentality was, "I just don't catch breaks, so why would I catch a break?" I needed to have control of others because of the uncertainty surrounding something being taken from me. The truth was, I needed to get control of myself. My flaws kept me from doing a lot of great things. They were overpowering me, and I had to set new boundaries. The time was now to replace the old limitations with fresh, more promising beliefs of myself.

OK. I know where all of my insecurities originated, and why I didn't feel like I was worth a damn. But I had to set the discomfort aside. I didn't forget about it, but I needed to seek out and analyze where I was having success. Any little successes, if you will, mattered! They showed me that I wasn't a complete fuck-up all the time. I thought of things that I was already good at, that I wasn't giving myself credit for. Simple things, for example: I am a safe driver (I drive like a grandpa). This was something I was good at, and so was taking my life seriously when I was sober, or how I played sports. I was talented enough to play college baseball; many players never get past high school. Or how about me being friendly with people? This was a definite success in my life. Or how about that I take good care of others? This was another success in my life.

Before I knew it, I had built up a nice list. It was part of the solution for me establishing my worth again. My worth was something I was going to set for myself, and I'd be damned if another person would design that for me. I was on a mission to figure it out. I had been stationing my worth on incorrect measurements: how much money I made, how many compliments I got, what my job title was…all of which had zero impact on my value and worth. It was a sheer mix up. My insecurities were dominating me, so now I had to trust that I was made exactly the way I was for a reason, and that my life up to this point had me going in the direction I need to be going. I had to tell myself over and over and over again that I was capable of being the man I had always wanted to be, or sell myself a new story, if you will. A good, loving story.

The excuses were over. I had to forgive others and forgive myself. Blaming was not getting me anywhere. I had to learn to keep up with myself and live the life I wanted to live. I was not in competition with anyone. I was put in this world to create, and I am here to do what I want to do! Worrying about what others were doing or had done was a terrible habit I had to get rid of, just so I could start to see myself as a confident and comfortable person. It was all already inside of me, but somehow it had been buried under many years of shit.

I had been taught that the most important job I would ever have was to know and learn about myself. And that, in the process, I would like myself for who I really was and discover that I was fully capable, talented, and unique, neither inferior nor superior because no two humans are identical. I started to appreciate the gifts I was given. I had to give up judgment of others because that meant I had a low opinion of myself. I was trying to put people down to make myself feel better to get on top, a solution I had distanced myself from for a long time. The word esteem means to appreciate the worth of. I was on a rampage to show more appreciation for others, "Hey, dude, I know you're awesome. If not, well, you are a human, so I appreciate you!" I would tell people this, even strangers sometimes. I had to teach myself to treat other people as if they were of some value and, in return, I would feel appreciation for myself.

I figured out who I was, what I stood for, and how I should behave and believe that no person would get in the way of my actions. They were not going to throw me off course. I had a goal in mind and it was to find my worth. It was my job to stay in command of myself and my behavior. I was going to act on, and not simply respond to, the ignorant behavior of others. I had to become the master of my actions and attitude.

Believe it: Everyone starts life with a healthy dose of self-worth and self-value, but that can change during the growing years. Mine was the result of several different events. If you lack the value you seek, it's likely because you don't know who you really are just yet. In this discovery, you will strike gold! Our rock-the-cradle years have an enormous pop on our self-worth. If you came from a struggling family, as I did, there are often limits and difficulties in understanding that self-worth comes from action, doing the right thing, something, anything, over and over again, despite the original outcome. As they say, some decision is better than no decision. Start admiring and aspiring. Take baby steps and, most importantly, make an investment to master your life. It's your number one priority and the most rewarding work you will ever do.

PART FOUR:
THE PRESENT

Chapter 15
A Moment of Mindfulness

"The best way to capture moments is to pay attention. This is how we cultivate mindfulness. Mindfulness means being awake. It means knowing what you are doing."

—*Jon Kabat-Zinn*

Have you ever met someone and, immediately after the meeting, forgotten the person's name? Then the following inner dialogue begins. "Come on, man, What was her name again? Was it Teri? No…it was Tori? Ah, that doesn't sound right. It is Kira? No, maybe it was Sara? Gosh, I have no idea!…No, I got it…It's Tara! Sorry, wrong again." Now imagine you added three, four, five extra people to the mix. How can you possibly remember everyone's name?

It is not because your memory sucks; it's definitely not because you are not smart enough, or that you aren't a loving person. It has everything to do with you not being mindful. Did you stop paying attention on purpose? If so, you are missing the moment, the moment where everything is happening right now. Where are your listening skills at this given time? Distractions will kill the opportunities to seize the moment! Being mindful is not a matter of judging good from bad or right from wrong as an event is happening. The goal is to slow down the brain chitchat and digress from the normal patterns that control your behavior. Allow yourself to feel the moment, the present.

How about your regular drive to the office, Monday through Friday, each morning of every week? Do you remember the quest? Most people could not tell you one detail about the time spent driving. Why is that? Well, in our modern society, we have gotten used to juggling too many tasks at once. While you are driving, you are searching through your iPhone to see who you have to e-mail to meet work deadlines; you are on the phone at the same time with your secretary, scheduling the afternoon meetings; you are trying to adjust the volume of the radio because it is too loud; and you are trying to change the station and find a better song, because Taylor Swift just came on and you can't stand her! We are in autopilot and our habits have taken over.

"Dude, you are losing control of the moment. Wake up, wake up! Get right here with me! Right here! Be totally present with me!

While I was going through my coaching training for social and emotional intelligence, I was taught, and had to understand (for the coach, who was me, that I must pay full attention to what the client is bringing to the table, and what they are saying. I have to be aware, attentive, and not pass criticism. Mindfulness is a skill that can be developed. These same rules apply for anyone, even if you are not a coach. Acceptance of what is gives you an advantage over managing problems. Mindfulness teaches us a way of being rather than doing. Here are some truths I learned in some additional studies, wherein I not only paid attention to myself for myself, but also expressed such sentiments to my clients.

Mindfulness improves well-being:

- Increasing your capacity for mindfulness supports many attitudes that contribute to a satisfied life.

- Being mindful makes it easier to savor the pleasures in life as they occur, helps you become fully engaged in activities, and creates a greater capacity to deal with adverse events.

- By focusing on the here and now, many people who practice mindfulness find that they are less likely to get caught up in worries about the future or regrets over the past, are less preoccupied with concerns about success and self-esteem, and are better able to form deep connections with others.

Mindfulness improves physical health. If greater well-being isn't enough of an incentive, scientists have discovered that the benefits of mindfulness techniques help improve physical health in a number of ways.

Mindfulness can:

- help relieve stress

- treat heart disease

- lower blood pressure

- reduce chronic pain

- improve sleep

- alleviate gastrointestinal difficulties

Mindfulness improves mental health. In recent years, psychotherapists have turned to mindfulness meditation as an important element in the treatment of a number of problems, including:

- depression

- substance abuse

- eating disorders

- couples' conflicts

- anxiety disorders

- obsessive-compulsive disorder

Legendary basketball coach Phil Jackson won a total of eleven NBA championships, six titles with the Chicago Bulls, five with the Los Angeles Lakers, and two as a player back in the 1970s for the New York Knicks. He coached two of the greatest players of all time, who often show up in topics of conversation about who the best basketball player of all time is. Michael

Jordan or Kobe Bryant? Despite what the answer may be, Coach Jackson had a technique, a strategy, and, as he points out in an interview with Oprah Winfrey, he had to master another critical element in order to reach their level of success. It wasn't just about being the best basketball players, lifting the most weights, and being the fastest team on the court. While all those things can certainly provide an advantage, Jackson wanted his team to use other tactics.

This is their conversation during episode 424 of Super Soul Sunday.

> Oprah: "One of the things that you knew you had to do with the Bulls in the beginning here in Chicago and then moving on to the Lakers, especially with Kobe Bryant. You knew you had to create a team, you had to build a team, and one of the ways you did that was with the one-breath, one-mind. Can you explain how? And what did the guys think of you coming in with your Zen stuff?

> Phil: "Laughs…"

> Oprah: "Here you are…"

> Phil: "I never coached it in Zen stuff. You know I approached it with mindfulness."

> Oprah: "Mindfulness. Yes."

> Phil: "You know a lot of our players in the NBA are from deeply religious families, very much like my background. And anything that would be a conflict

to their religious beliefs I didn't want to touch or get them upset about it. And so…"

Oprah: "Isn't it interesting how you knew that because you come from that?"

Phil: "Exactly."

Oprah: "Yes."

Phil: "So we talked about mindfulness as being as much as we pump iron, and we run to build our strength up, we need to build our mental strength up. We need to build our mental strength so we can focus, get one point at attention, and so that we can be in concert with one another in times of need. When you come off the court, you've had a bad call, things are going wrong for you, you sit on the bench, you take a breath, and you reseat yourself, you reset yourself. And you do that through this mindfulness, you just come right back in and collect yourself. So we practiced mindfulness, which you have to do."

Oprah: "So, you would literally have the guys sit in stillness?"

Phil: "That's right."

Oprah: "Meditating?"

Phil: "That's right."

Phil: "Taught them how to hold their hands, where their shoulders had to be, the whole process of being in upright situations so that you're not slouched and you're not going to fall asleep. And they bought into it."

Oprah: "Would you do this before every game? You would do this regularly? You would do this..."

Phil: "We introduced it, and we introduced it in training camp, and then day of games we started using, and it ultimately became a process where..."

Oprah: "It's like centering yourself."

Phil: "That's right, just getting back and being centered."

Oprah: "Did you not also have them play in the dark at one point?"

Phil: "It wasn't totally dark, but I wanted them to get the idea of being able to do things that are just out of the ordinary. Like silence day, have a day of just silence. There is a lot of chatter in basketball, and rightfully, you want players to be talking to each other and communicating with each other, but sometimes at practice it gets too verbose and guys are yelling and having fun with each other and teasing each other. So I tried to take things out of the ordinary and make them something special so they'd understand the difference."

Oprah: "And so were the guys receptive in the beginning to these new ideas about mindfulness and being able to master the game from the inner?"

Phil: "Yeah. I think they tolerated it, and I think the reason why they tolerated it, this is one of the things I talk about in the book, is about being authentic, and coming from who you are and what you think is important. I mean, you know, Oprah, I tried tai chi with the players, they were doing tai chi, and we tried yoga, we tried a bunch of things that didn't stick. The players were like you know, um, I'm too tired after practice to do yoga, you know, I've got tendinitis in the knee. I can't get in the position that's right for tai chi. But I wanted to give them opportunities to explore some of those things. But what did stick was meditation. That was always something that was able to stick with these guys."

Oprah: "So powerful. And then you move on to the Lakers. Were your mindfulness practices as embraced as they had been in Chicago?"

Phil: "You know I think those guys would have laid down and let me run on top of them or something when I first got there. They were very, very receptive. Um, there was hiccups along the way without a doubt, but as far as being willing learners with an open mind, they were very accommodating for me, and I am very gracious and glad about that."

Oprah: "You actually say in the book that you know driving a basketball down the court could be one of the most mundane, you know, day-to-day boring as you describe it, activities, but being able to find the sacred in that."

Phil: "Yes, to put spirit into it, you have to get spirit back into things."

Oprah: "Yeah."

So what does this mean? It means that mindfulness is for everyone. Anyone can enjoy the benefits. Ask yourself these two questions:

What did I learn from that conversation? And how can I begin to foster mindfulness?

Mindfulness gives life to our emotions. When mind and body are in alignment, we can feel the moment. In this moment, we can see and feel all the components of happiness. It comes so easily. So naturally. We don't have to wait to feel the bliss. It is always present inside of us, right here, right now! It's just a few simple attitude adjustments away from being accessed.

Although I do not use meditation as a form of mindfulness, it is strongly encouraged as part of the process of becoming more mindful. It is a method of helping you focus your attention. I have used some other techniques that have worked well for me. I farm my own mindfulness by focusing my attention singularly, from moment to moment, and being aware of my feelings over the course of the day, which includes all activities. By singularly, I mean doing one thing at a time, and giving it my full attention: typing on the computer, making my breakfast, taking a shower, or writing a sentence for this chapter. For each, I am fully present and, because of that, life slows down for me. All of my attention is congruent with all of my senses.

My other favorites are straight from Alfred James. I use these techniques on a daily basis, and he describes the exercises best in his blog.

MINDFUL OBSERVATION

This exercise is simple but incredibly powerful. It is designed to connect us with the beauty of the natural environment, something that is easily missed when we are rushing around in the car or hopping on and off trains on the way to work. Choose a natural object from within your immediate environment and focus on watching it for a minute or two. This could be a flower or an insect, or even the clouds or the moon. Don't do anything except notice the thing you are looking at. Simply relax into a harmony for as long as your concentration allows. Look at it as if you are seeing it for the first time. Visually explore every aspect of its formation. Allow yourself to be consumed by its presence. Allow yourself to connect with its energy and its role and purpose in the natural world.

MINDFUL AWARENESS

This exercise is designed to cultivate a heightened awareness and appreciation of simple daily tasks and the results they achieve. Think of something that happens every day more than once; something you take for granted—like opening a door, for example. At the very moment you touch the doorknob to open the door, stop for a moment, and be mindful of where you are, how you feel in that moment, and where the door will lead you. Similarly, the moment you open your computer to start work, take a moment to appreciate the hands that enable this process and the brain that facilitates your understanding of how to use the computer. These touch-point cues don't have to be physical ones. For example: Each time you think a negative thought, you might choose to take a moment to stop, label the thought as unhelpful, and release the negativity. Or, perhaps each time you smell food, you take a moment to stop and appreciate how lucky you are to have good food to eat and share with your family and friends.

Choose a touch point that resonates with you today. Instead of going through your daily motions on autopilot, take occasional moments to stop and cultivate purposeful awareness of what you are doing and the blessings your actions brings to your life.

MINDFUL LISTENING

This exercise is designed to open your ears to sound in a nonjudgmental way. So much of what we see and hear on a daily basis is influenced by our past experiences, but when we listen mindfully, we achieve a neutral, present awareness that lets us hear sound without preconception. Select a piece of music you have never heard before. You may have something in your own collection that you have never listened to, or you might choose to turn the radio dial until something catches your ear. Close your eyes and put on your headphones. Try not to be drawn into judging the music by its genre, title, or artist name before it has begun playing. Instead, ignore any labels and neutrally allow yourself to get lost in the journey of sound for the duration of the song. Allow yourself to explore every aspect of the track. Even if the music isn't to your liking at first, let go of your dislike and give your awareness full permission to climb inside the track and dance among the sound waves. The idea is to just listen, to become fully entwined with the composition without preconception or judgment of the genre, artist, lyrics, or instrumentation.

Here is the great news. Mindfulness can be integrated into your daily routine. Even if you are a busy person, you can start to practice mindfulness. Day to day there is an opportunity for you to work on the practices and techniques of mindfulness. It doesn't require a huge time block; in fact, you can work on it moment to moment. The principles are always the same. I suggest getting in tune with what is exactly happening, in the now, in the moment. It is our job to be present. Being conscious every step of the way will give you a greater level of satisfaction. Take notice of your surroundings and the way you feel the minute you kick-start your day. Your rituals should appear much clearer to you. The movements, the smells, the noises you hear, the way your breath tastes after eating your bagel and cream cheese. Allow your senses to be fully engaged through all of the sensations that life is granting you. Get in your car and notice the temperature inside the vehicle, check in with what you feel when you turn on the ignition, listen to the sound come through the speakers. Pay attention on the journey. Leave the distractions behind. Notice the streets, the cars driving alongside you, the number of red lights you hit, your walk into the office building, the ride up the elevator. Be so in touch with the moment and notice that it's a beautiful feeling.

I was living insensibly for my whole life. I didn't know what it meant to live in the moment before discovering the mindful approach and the benefits I would access in a whole new dimension of life, which included: my own thoughts, feelings, sensations, objects, and environments, which I was experiencing minute by minute. The goal is to embrace these experiences. Allow them to enter your conscious awareness, and then allow them to remove themselves without judgment. Here we can get lost in our awareness, but not lose our attention. Mindfulness is a working discipline where, the more you practice it, the more effect it will end up having on your overall joy. Being mindful will help stretch and strengthen the natural functions of the mind from the purest point of existence.

Chapter 16
Living on Purpose

"If your life is cloudy, and you're far, far off course, then you may have to go on faith for a while, but eventually you'll learn that every time you trust your internal navigation system, you end up closer to your right life."

—*Martha Beck*

"Manny, get up...get up...Hey boy! Get your ass up!" This was my dad at 3:00 a.m.

"What do you want?" I would say angrily.

"Don't you have to go to work in an hour?"

"Don't remind me, please, as if it's not already bad enough I work at this shithole. Maybe I'll just miss the whole day and not tell anyone."

And that's exactly what I did for my food and beverage manager position. I got five, then ten, then twenty calls because people were concerned and, finally, when I wanted to talk to them, I told them my phone was missing. How professional of me, right? How many jobs have you had where you've dreaded waking up, getting ready, and working through the day? You know in your heart something is missing, and you can feel the absence in your life of pleasure, passion, excitement, and clarity.

Well, what is stopping you from getting up and moving in a different direction?

I know! Fear. Doubt. You're comfortable. It pays the bills. If you leave, you won't know what to do next because the work you are doing now is all you know, and let me tell you, I have been there! I need four hands and four feet to count all of the times I called off work, or just didn't go because I was disgusted with the duties.

Still, it's a job! Yay! I think this is why I loved sales so much, because I could work from home with nobody bothering me. This profession was an excuse for me to be a lazy ass, just before I would realize I was just going through the motions. I never enjoyed any of the work I did. Over the course of several jobs, I would come up with every excuse and objection humanly possible. I was constantly arguing for my limitations, and guess what? I got to keep them. You are not a tree! Therefore, it is your job to get up and move when you are unhappy with your conditions.

For ten years, I tried and failed, tried and failed. I thought I was getting closer to reaching a point in my life where I would find a reason for being, a job that would give me status, and a big paycheck. But in every circumstance, my time was short-lived. Jobs- I was either fired or I would quit; sometimes, I would leave for other "opportunities." I was in and out of relationships and dating. "I'll never find the one," I thought. "Ugh. Is it worth it to keep moving forward?"

Without a doubt, the answer was yes. I went to hell and back several times over, and now I am here, writing, on purpose. I didn't quit, although I seriously considered giving up on life several times. I didn't let the failures of my life continue to sideline me, because I wanted to be the star player on my own team, and serve others, respectively.

Sadly, many people give up on themselves way too early in life, leaving a lifetime of potential sitting just underneath their skin. Just getting by is not the way life is supposed to be lived. My point is, live from a point of courage, be unreasonable, make a difference, take risks. Your dreams are never too distant to reach out and grab them, and you are never too old or too young to bring them to life either.

Think about your childhood and people asking what you wanted to be when you grew up.

"Manny, what do you want to be when you grow up?"

"A baseball player!"

"Joe, how about you?"

"A singer!"

"Susie, and you, pumpkin?"

"I want to be a musician, just like my momma."

"Terry, I see you sitting quietly over there. What's your dream job?"

"I want to get the bad guys!"

"Oh, so you want to be a policeman?"

"Yep!"

"David, what's your dream for when you get older?"

"I want to cut people open. My dad says it's a lot of fun!"

"So you mean like a doctor?"

"Yeah!"

Do any of these ring a bell? Of course they do, but we got lost in the shuffle of life, and about what it means to dream. We were pushed into this idea of living a life where everyone wants us to live according to their plan. Spending your time doing anything less than what you love is a complete waste of time. It is so important to remember that you qualify, that you are capable, capable of doing everything you have ever dreamed of. Why not treat yourself to everything your heart desires? It's only fair to you to be your best self, not just when you dress up for an event, or go on a date, but all the stinking time!

A few months ago, I had to prepare a talk for a group of seniors. They were all pushing age sixty or seventy. I thought to myself, "How in the world am I going to get these folks on board with my message when they've lived out their life already?" And then it hit me. It didn't matter that I was thinking; they had all of the answers already, on what their situation was. What mattered was that there is always room to discover more about yourself and do more of what you love. Not everyone has the answer. Sometimes you find your purpose early, sometimes you find it late. It is only too late, though, when you are underground. We have a personal responsibility to always be working toward something, so if you find yourself struggling with the "it's too late" idea, stop it. Don't count yourself out.

How many of you remember this one? I mean, this was personal. This city was let down time and time again as it wiped tears away, year after year, getting so close to breaking the curse. How much money did they spend to bring the most talented pitchers and position players available? Every press conference was another empty promise on delivering a championship. These players, the organization, and the city were one; they were like a family. So when they conquered this unimaginable curse, they were able to raise the victory flag high, over a town that just been given a breath of fresh air before they were at it again the next season. Matt Yoder writes about it best on the comeback blog, GO SOX! "The greatest comeback in sports history was just three outs from never happening. But when the Red

Sox came back from a 4–3 deficit in the bottom of the ninth in game four of the 2004 ALCS to win in extras, they began a journey that we'd never experienced before or since. The Red Sox went on to win game five, game six, and game seven to complete the impossible. When we add on top of that comeback the intensity of the Yankees-Red Sox rivalry, the Curse of the Bambino, the Bloody Sock, walk-off victories, and everything else in that crazy series, it's a once-in-a-lifetime event that we were all privileged to witness, and the greatest comeback in sports history…unless you're a Yankees fan, that is."

Three outs are easy to get, right? Not so. The tide can turn in baseball quickly. A team can be down in a game with their backs to the wall in the bottom of the ninth, facing defeat, or in this case elimination. They needed to win four straight games, and then four more during the World Series to come out and win the championship. What makes this any different from your life? Can you make your life take the same turn and win against all odds? Sure, you can! The odds are only the odds on a big LED screen in the sport books on Las Vegas Boulevard. Once again, it's never too late to cultivate your gifts, your talents, and to change the course of your life, much like the Red Sox changed the trajectory of their season in 2004.

Finding your purpose is an inside job, but you must discover it. Some people are supposed to be writers, teachers, coaches, or speakers, but they never figure this out! You will not find it anywhere outside of yourself.

You must start with a vision, which is born in your imagination. Your purpose is why you get up every day. Your purpose is your reason for living. Take some time and ask yourself: "What do I really love doing?" Go find a quiet area in a park, in nature, at the peak of a mountain, and let the mind be free. Leave the phone behind, just bring a pen and paper so you can write down everything it is that you enjoy. Find the time for an escape, to find peace and quiet. If you could spend your life doing something, what would it be? Draw out and write down this ideal life of yours. If you want to have a house on the beach and work from home, I'll ask you, "Why do you think you can't have this?" Surprise, *you can*! What are you going to leave behind? What is the legacy you want to be remembered for? How can you get people to think about you long after you are gone? When you start to work on discovering your purpose, you'll be subject to a steady flow of new ideas. So be prepared—it's a joyous feeling. You have one chance at life, the life you want, one life, and it doesn't wait up for anyone. The clock keeps on ticking, so make sure you find the time to work on discovering your purpose. You owe it to yourself.

If you were to ask people, "What do you want?" they will struggle to give you one answer. But ask them to tell you what they don't want, and they will spit off an infinite list of items in a millisecond the minute you ask them. Having a vision will help you deliver on your purpose. There might be a multitude of things you want to accomplish over a lifetime. It is your duty to spend time thinking about, questions like, "How can I do things better? How can I give more?" Keeping a long-range image of everything you want to do helps bring your purpose into focus.

I want to stress the importance of being clear and specific on your vision and desire. If you don't know, that's OK. But don't dance around the idea; otherwise, you'll always put it off and vainly hope it comes to you. It won't. You have to do the work to find yourself. If you make one exception, that soon turns into two, then three, and then life becomes the exception. Try out as many things as you can, on one condition: Accept that you will fail, and that the answer will come in due time. It's a feeling and you will know. Life will simplify because of it, and your dream will be much easier to accomplish when you know exactly what it is you want. Cutting off all other possibilities and having a clear and specific vision will transform your life!

So how do you bring the purpose and the vision together? By setting goals. Our uniqueness emerges when we set lofty goals. Goals are direction and they give you the roadmap for arriving at your destination. Goals create your future in advance. It is about a process and who you become within that process. So why don't most people set goals? For several reasons. One legend of personal development, Zig Ziglar, points out in one audio recording, the four reasons why:

Fear

False Evidence Appearing Real. He says the average 18-year-old has been told 148,000 times "no" or "you can't do it."

Poor self-image

Individuals cannot imagine becoming college grads, getting a good job, having a nice home, being financially successful.

Never been sold

The mind is always traveling and that is the reason why people say they don't have enough time. The state of mind is always crossing work and play.

People don't know how

It takes time to write down realistic goals for all areas of your life but, once you do it, you will gain additional time in the future to pursue all of your real interests. Like your purpose.

I have helped construct hundreds of vacations, and I have been a vital part of the planning process for trips, particularly to Las Vegas, where people take great care in their travel arrangements. Well-planned via time spent on the phone and back-and-forth text messaging, they spend hours of their time. What shocks me is that people spend more time planning to come out to Las

Vegas to party, get wasted, and forget an evening than they do in planning the direction of their lives. Why is that? Maybe it's because it is easier to escape than it is to challenge ourselves. Your goals are vital. I encourage you to write them down and get specific. Create short-range, midrange, and long-range goals. It is useless to set goals if you do not take action on them daily. How will you make this all come together? Write it down!

Get lost in the journey toward your dreams. If you set a goal and you know how to reach it, then you are not setting large enough goals. Your goals should scare this piss out of you. It's OK that you don't know how to reach them right now, just *know that you will get there with absolute certainty.* There is much more to life than nice cars, plaques, medals, or anything else materialistic. People get more lost in reaching the outcome than they do in who they become in the process. The extrinsic rewards only provide so much satisfaction, and it is often temporary. Great results are exciting, but they are distractions from what our true intentions are. Connect yourself to making a difference, and be in tune with what you love to do. The value in finding your purpose is that it allows you to be flexible and to sway with the changes in your life because you are operating from your heart. Stop waiting for the time to be right; it will never be the perfect time. The key is to get in the game. Wait and you'll miss the boat of life. Life is not promised, but death is. Once you understand this, you'll find joy in each passing day and share your gift with others. It's time.

Chapter 17
All You Need Is Love

"Love all, trust a few, do wrong to none."

—*William Shakespeare*

Do you know what love is? How would you explain it? How can you separate puppy love from a deep craving to be whole with another person?

Or is it something that is very difficult to explain and instead an emotion that is best described as a feeling. Every person will have a different answer for this topic. It is what makes us unique. Sure, there are definitions and articles to follow and read, but that can only provide us a way of *understanding* more about what love really is.

But what if you, like me, found it very difficult to understand the meaning of love for the majority of life? I know I fooled myself into believing I was in love during some relationships, just to make myself feel better. I was lying with my words, even though there was one exception—a woman I dated who, without a doubt, had all of my heart. Love is an emotion that I can't explain. It is a strong feeling, and I know this much: I am battling myself right now to lay it on the line, but I think I'd rather talk about some of the education I got on the subject so I can use it for a better human experience, and love openly, as my life moves forward. The old way wasn't working out. If love hurts and it's the only thing you know, then trust it; if it makes you feel alive, then latch onto the power.

Truthfully, it's my personal belief that most of us only associate love with our romantic partners because we want long-lasting marriage love. The more homework and research I did, the more articles I read that were related to "partners" and "romantic relationships." However, there are more areas of love, and the meaning can have a powerful impact on the quality of your life. Let's check out how the Greeks described it. I found the best version of an explanation in the online article below. The information stuck with me because I could understand the differences very clearly.

Consider how you feel for the people you are close to while pondering the four types of love listed below.

AGAPE

This is an unconditional love that sees beyond the outer surface and accepts the recipient for whom he/she is, regardless of their flaws, shortcomings or faults. It's the type of love that everyone strives to have for their fellow human beings. Although you may not like someone, you decide to love them just as a human being. This kind of love is all about sacrifice as well as giving and expecting nothing in return. The translation of the word agape is love in the verb form: it is the love demonstrated by your behavior toward another person. It is a committed and chosen love.

PHILEO

The phileo love refers to an affectionate, warm and tender platonic love. It makes you desire friendship with someone. It's the kind of love which livens up the agape love. Although you may have an agape love for your enemies, you may not have a phileo love for the same people. The translation of the word phileo is love in the noun form: it is how you feel about someone. It is a committed and chosen love.

STORGE

It is a kind of family and friendship love. This is the love that parents naturally feel for their children; the love that members of the family have for each other; or the love that friends feel for each other. In some cases, this friendship love may turn into a romantic relationship, and the couple in such a relationship becomes best friends. storge love is unconditional, accepts flaws or faults and ultimately drives you to forgive. It's committed, sacrificial and makes you feel secure, comfortable and safe.

EROS

Eros is a passionate and intense love that arouses romantic feelings; it is the kind that often triggers "high" feelings in a new relationship and makes you say, "I love him/her." It is simply an emotional and sexual love. Although this romantic love is important in the beginning of a new relationship, it may not last unless it moves a notch higher because it focuses more on self instead of the other person. If the person "in love" does not feel good about their relationship anymore, they will stop loving their partner."

I am going to be blunt here. I never understood love until I went on my expedition and decided I wanted to feel the heavens. I started to use the word more effectively because I took it upon myself to study the meaning. I knew that if I didn't open up my heart to let the love in, I would continue to suffer. Love is learned and love is progressive interaction. We design our knowledge and lack thereof, again, in childhood. Our love intake is created by spending time around someone long enough to absorb their love, rather than by a decision and conscious creation.

I had the hardest time telling my father, the rest of my family, and my friends that I loved them. Why? I was scared. It was the only way I knew how to deal; nor did I hear it very often growing up. I am not blaming anyone. It just so happens that, although I know I was loved, I wasn't frequently reminded during my upbringing. I can now choose to leave the pain in the past. When I would speak of love, I always gave my best quick version—"love ya"; not "I love you," but "love ya," as if it was easing the difficulty of saying it. My behavior was an accurate reflection of who I was and what I was feeling on the inside. If I didn't love myself, how in the heck was I going to love others? But I figured it out. If I was unsure of my feelings, then saying, "I love you" was like agreeing to drink the disgusting medicine dad tried serving me when I was sick. "No! I don't want it." I had to detach from the notion that I was too "tough" for love. The idea was that, if I were to say "love," it didn't make me feel weak. I wasn't a homosexual if I said "I love you" to my male friends. It wasn't awkward to say it to my dad. I think of the storge love now. Unconditional! My dad is my dad! Of course, I love him! And now I know he loves me! *Dad, I love you sooo much! You are my rock, my best friend and I am proud to have you as my father!*

Clearly you stay away from acknowledging every new person in your life with an "I love you." But if you feel it between you and a closely connected relative or friend, say it! It's healthy to let it out and let people know they influence your beating heart. Never give love up. It is a constant state of being. Those who block it out of their life don't stand a fighting chance against life's most challenging obstacles. I had to agree to understand the power behind it. It was time to get rid of my negative responses to love.

In Robert Firestone's article, I learned that

"Being loved arouses anxiety because it threatens long-standing psychological defenses formed early in life in relation to emotional pain and rejection, therefore leaving a person feeling more vulnerable. Although the experience of being chosen and especially valued is exciting and can bring happiness and fulfillment, at the same time, it can be frightening and the fear often translates into anger and hostility. Basically, love is scary when it contrasts with childhood trauma. In that situation, the beloved feels compelled to act in ways that hurt the lover: behaving in a punitive manner, distancing themselves and pushing love away. In essence, people maintain the defensive posture that they formed early in life. Because the negative reaction to positive events occurs without conscious awareness, individuals respond without understanding what caused them to react. They rationalize the situation by finding fault with or blaming others, particularly those closest to them."

Does this ring a bell? For me it does. When momma died, I closed the door on love, permanently. That was my ghastly childhood trauma. My mom and dad were not in love after an early divorce, a process I surely witnessed. And I am sure he also closed the door on love, a move that was passed on to me. How could I trust anyone to love me if my own mother disappeared on me? It was a vicious battle for a long time. And now it all makes sense. Zen Buddhist teacher Thich Nhat Hanh says, "If our parents didn't love and understand each other, how are we to know what love looks like?

The most precious inheritance that parents can give their children is their own happiness. Our parents may be able to leave us money, houses, and land, but they may not be happy people. If we have happy parents, we have received the richest inheritance of all."

It is important to understand the changing emotions you feel as you use the word love to describe them. Saying things like "I love my job" might actually mean "I really enjoy coming to work." "I love my bed" might actually mean, "I appreciate a good night's rest." "I love that movie" might actually mean you value the hard work it took to produce it. "I love myself"…excellent, you're worth it! "I love my life!" Fuck yeah, you earned it!

Knowing the real meaning of words is invaluable to your literacy of love because words are strong tools. They help you communicate more effectively with others and yourself. The words used build an awareness and manifests your reality. By using caution with your words, you can be more conscious of the type of love you are feeling. If you have enough understanding and love, then every moment, whether it's spent cooking, washing the car, or cleaning the house, can be a moment of joy.

If you don't understand love, you can't love. Real true love exists in kindness, compassion, joy, and equality. Love is the most powerful emotion we experience. So why not have the deepest possible understanding of love if it can have the greatest influence on us? Sometimes common sense isn't always common practice. It's your job to do the work.

Chapter 18
Finding Fulfillment

"Life is a promise, fulfill it."

—*Mother Teresa*

So I'm sitting at my desk, starting this last chapter, when I came across a rather interesting fact. I wanted to leave fulfillment for the conclusion because it has everything to do with satisfaction and happiness—a derivative of developing one's ability or character, as said in its definition. My original idea was to begin the first sentence of this chapter with the date I booked what has been the most memorable, joyful, and adventurous trip of my life—until this point. But when I pulled up my e-mail history to check the records of the date I purchased the airline ticket, for that trip, I shockingly read November 9, the same day I came to "the discovery," on a Monday, several months before, sitting in a work meeting. I was going through a reality check, three days after making a decision to stop drinking. I never imagined I would come so far!

After I clicked the purchase-ticket button, I phoned my friends to tell them I was booked for a trip. I immediately began making a list of activities I wanted to do. Places I wanted to see. Foods I wanted to try. And bridges I wanted to cross. And the greatest part? My friends Harold and Henry were excited to receive me and show me around. My friend Chris was traveling from Los Angeles to come spend time also. How could I not already be in a state of total appreciation? Henry was going to let me stay at his place for the first half of the trip, and I would rent a shared Airbnb with three complete strangers for the second half of my stay. I've never stayed with three strangers before, but I was expanding my person. I wanted to force myself to grow by trying the unknown. It was my first time to the city, and the hype was stratospheric. January 14 was my departure date, and I was going to be there for one week. I had no expectations. I was so damn happy, that's all. I was on the red eye flying into Charlotte first, changing planes, and then off to my final destination, taking on seven hours and minutes' worth of travel time.

The same week, I was running around, shopping for cold gear! I didn't own anything more than a windbreaker and some jeans. I was from the blistering hot city of Vegas. My inventory of snowy clothing was really low. I was told, "It's going to be bone-chilling cold, it's so cold here already. January is freezing. Are you crazy?" Maybe, but I didn't mind. I was ready to explore and traverse. No rain, snow, or freezing cold temperatures would stop me.

The evening of my red-eye flight I packed my bags to the brim. Three new puffy winter coats filled the luggage. I wasn't sure if I would be able to fit my boxers, shirts, pants, and so forth. But after using my fancy Tetris skills and all of my muscle, I managed to get the luggage to zip up. What a great feeling. I had a second carryon bag with a few pairs of shoes, my laptop, and journals with all of my Happiness notes and goals. I had a new habit of constantly reminding myself of what matters most in life. Those notes read:

Happiness lies within self. Happy people function better, feel better, are more productive, healthier, and live a longer life.

Social bonding, social interaction, and cooperation are rewarding intrinsically to human beings. We are social creatures and the act of cooperation with another human being can feel just as good as a drug.

Joy comes from a connection to others.

Count your blessings. Acts of kindness.

The good news is that the things we love to do are the building block of a happy life.

- *Play*

- *Having new experiences*

- ***Friends and family***

- ***Doing things that are meaningful***

- ***Appreciating what we have***

And they are free. And with the more happiness I have, the more happiness everyone has!

When I arrived at McCarran International Airport and passed through security, I took the tram over to the D-gates to locate D-whatever jet way I was leaving from and wait for my American Airlines flight. I decided to stop in the Hudson News store beforehand because I needed to pick up a few things. Hmm, which book do I want to get? Oh, oh, oh, and a selfie stick! My first one.

"Excuse me, but where are the selfie sticks?" I asked.

"Here, we have a cheap one or the expensive one."

"My first one ever!" I told the clerk, with a bundle of excitement backing my words, that I had no idea what I was getting myself into. Forty dollars later, I had a new toy and a brand new book to read. I was determined to keep pushing the muscles of my brain because learning was now fun, and this long, cross-country trip would be the perfect opportunity to educate myself more. After all, this was one of the building blocks of my happiness. I was all about doing now. *Action.* I was getting such a high in stretching myself to new academic heights that it would be silly not to have an open book every down minute I had. I was very clear on what was making me happy, and that was apparent now. *Productivity!* It was a 180-degree turn for my life from a few months before.

"Sir? Can you fasten your seatbelt, put away the tray table, and sit back in the upright and locked position?

"Oh yes, I'm sorry."

I was already several chapters deep into my book with laser focus. And guess what? I had the whole row to myself. Now, was I lucky or what? No. I'm convinced I *earned* the freedom, and this was just the start. I was doing everything right; God was giving me the legroom I deserved, literally.

Two hours into our flying time, I finally pulled my nose out of the book. I was suspended, thirty-five thousand feet up, in a giant tin can. How awesome is that! I was reading, highlighting, and taking notes. When I looked around the cabin to see if there was any movement, there was nothing. I could hear only the engines of the plane and see in front of me the dark cabin tunnel. I was the only one awake. My reading light was my companion. I asked myself, "Am I really the only one wide awake right now?" And I mean I was wide awake. It was impressive, considering I had been awake and running around for a full twenty-four hours before. I was on an internal mission and, with this observation, I got the chills, a body full of goosebumps. I wrote a note in my journal: "AA flight to Charlotte.

January 14, 2016. Everyone is completely asleep and I'm wide awake making my dream a reality, reading and writing my way to greatness!" Verbatim.

I knew that if I wanted to become someone I always dreamed of, I was going to have to do things I had never done before, and deciding to stay up and read versus taking a nap was a no-brainer. I embraced the truth here, and I was finding fulfillment in my life. The feeling wouldn't have indicated anything else. I felt cracked out, but this time it was not because I was high on cocaine or ecstasy. I was high on life, I was making progress, I was giving, and I was achieving!

I hit a sleepy wall when I landed in Charlotte. But a quick thirty-minute power nap to refresh got me back in my zone, and I was closer to arriving at my destination. Up, up, and away we went. I finished 90 percent of the book. I had never read a full book in anything less than a month, and in just five hours I was almost done reading this one during a flight across the United States. "Pretty cool," I thought. I was proud of myself. Once again, I was feeling inward satisfaction. By the time the flight attendant picked up her telephone and alerted us that we were about to start our descent, I started to feel the flow. The energy. The universe is full of it, and I was tapping into it completely. We were cruising over the outside lands of the city, but I couldn't see anything yet. My cheek was pressed against the window, looking out to get my first visual on what some people call the greatest city in the world. Yes, I was landing in New York City, the cultural and financial capital of the world! The power city! The concrete jungle! Home to the Empire State Building, Times Square, the Statue of Liberty, and other iconic sites! The top tourist attractions in the world! Manhattan! The Bronx! Brooklyn! Queens! This was my first time, and I thought to myself, "This place really does exist!"

All of my knowledge about New York was from outside sources. I didn't have my own personal experience there, yet. I had several friends who lived there and met many other great souls over the years who were from New York. I was from a cool place but I was always told, "New York has the upper hand over Las Vegas." I had seen it on TV, of course, when I was a kid watching Total Request Live from Times Square. I had seen it in all the newspapers, magazines, and movies—whether they were shooting the next big movie with the city skyline in the background- (The Wolf of Wall Street), or I was catching up on year's reruns of Christmas movies—Home Alone 2: Lost in New York—One of my favorites.

It's the home of the New York Yankees, who I grew up watching win championship after championship. And Madison Square Garden, where the iconic building hosts a multitude of events, including the Knicks and the Rangers in their respective sports. And the Empire State Building, where I fell in love with the scene from Sleepless in Seattle. How adorable. Tom Hanks finds his lost son and meets the lady his son set out to match him with, Meg Ryan. That's a romantic classic!

Here is the list I put together of places I wanted to see and things I wanted to do while I was in New York City:

- Staten Island Ferry (the Statue of Liberty)
- The Brooklyn Bridge/Coney Island
- Central Park
- Wall Street
- Financial District
- World Trade Center and 9/11 Museum
- Empire State Building
- Yankee Stadium
- Times Square
- Broadway
- Nets/Knicks game
- Grand Central Station
- Abetinos (to eat pizza)
- Brooklyn Heights Promenade
- South Street Seaport
- Rockefeller Center
- Battery Park
- Chrysler Building
- Met Museum
- Meat Packing District

- Washington Square Park
- Madison Square Garden

I was living in a prosperity world, and I was convinced I deserved to be having this experience in this abundant universe, that anything I ever wanted was available to me and at my fingertips. I was noticing prosperity everywhere. I had staggering opportunities to do things that were truly making me happy all at the same time. I was doing things I loved!

On the second day, I went on a stroll through Central Park. I had my selfie stick extended and phone hooked up to record and take photos. I had started on the north side of the park, and was walking south when I phoned my dad. I told him that had I arrived safely, but what I said next choked him up a little bit, and I could hear it. I said to him, "Dad I haven't always been able to give you very much because I have always been all over the place. I know lots of money would make things easier and, trust me, that is coming. But I figured out a way that I can pay you back for everything you have ever done for me, and that is to show you the way to being truly happy! I just want you to be happy! I can't wait to get home and talk with you about it!" I figured out how to be happy!

He was the first person I wanted to share this feeling with. It was now my role to make sure I carried this mission forward for my father. It was a magical revelation. I took the attention off myself, and shifted my interest to how can I spread this joy. I remember hanging up the phone, smiling ear to ear, and thinking to myself, "This is just the beginning." I continued on my walk. I passed the Harlem Meer, stopped, and took a 360-degree video of the city skyline at the reservoir. On my right was the Upper West Side neighborhood and, on my left, the Upper East Side. To the south, I could see the tip where the famed Plaza Hotel was on Fifth and Fifty-ninth. There were people everywhere. Bikers and runners were getting their morning cardio in. Tourists just like me were stopping and taking pictures every five minutes. Even the animals in the park were happy. I could see the smiles on their faces!

On day three, I took myself to a new dimension of possibility. After getting up early and taking the subway down to Wall Street, I met my friends, Chris and Erin, and we grabbed a bite to eat at the local bagel shop. The breakfast bagel I ordered was exploding with flavor. I was in New York, so I allowed myself a week of eating its foods—eggs, bacon, sausage, cheese, and lots of salt. It was totally necessary, as I was going to need the fuel for the remainder of the day. I was getting ready for a walkathon. First, we started our journey by walking over the Brooklyn Bridge. On that day, there were plenty of people with the same idea. I was dodging bikers, runners, and police buggies. The backdrop of the city skyline, with the One World Trade Center standing high above the surrounding skyscrapers, was spine chilling. The glare of the sun broke through the floating clouds and lit up the building. It looked surreal.

If there were ever a day I lived in New York, I would promise myself to make this walk part of my daily routine. When we arrived on the Brooklyn side, we stopped on the painted "Welcome to Brooklyn" street tag and took what was close to our hundredth group photo. And we had just began the trip forty-five minutes before. We were hoofing it. Each time, we looked at each other and said, "What's next?" I said, "*Let's. Keep. Going!*" My friends were really pleasured by showing me around. They both were former New Yorkers, so we zigzagged through the streets of Brooklyn, into the ritzy neighborhoods, where I got a little taste of the brick brownstone buildings I had seen in the movies and on TV. They were dark, earthy, and historic. I found excitement in the "never before seen in real life" concept.

In this wandering state of exploration, I approached a complete stranger on the street. The poor lady, carrying her grocery bags, was heading down the street in the same direction as we were, real close to the Brooklyn Promenade. I stopped her and asked for a picture. Why? Just because I wanted to share the moment. And I remembered that "joy comes from a connection to others." We got to chatting after the quick sidewalk photoshoot, and as it turned out, she was a spiritual healer and coach! This was so awesome. It was total and all-out divine connection. This was an area of life that I was very interested in now, since I was on my own spiritual journey. I asked a lot of questions! And I wanted to get to know her more, so I asked if we could get together and exchange stories while I was visiting. I was so curious, and so interested, in other human beings. Tell me more. I sent her this message on Sunday, January 17, at 3:34 p.m.

"Hi, Karen! This is Manny from yesterday walking in Brooklyn. I'd love to grab a coffee this week before I leave and talk with you about some of your work. I leave Thursday evening. Is there a good time for you?"

I was so fired up after this encounter for a few reasons:

— All of my *efforts* were being confirmed by the laws I was now studying. I was following the system for a more fulfilling life.

— I was just going for it. No more fear. Strictly confidence. I was enthusiastic to feel and be the change.

"Let's keep walking! Where are we headed to next?" I said to my friends. I could go all night at this speed, and I did. They must have thought I was crazy. This is the city that never slept, and I wasn't sleeping. We departed my new friend, Karen, and the Promenade area to head in the direction of the Barclays Center. By foot. More walking. Yay! We spent the least amount of time at the arena, but I wanted to get some quality photos. I am the sports guy, and I always feel a sense of pleasure in seeing the stadiums, arenas, and facilities the pros play in. Growing up, it was my dream to be a professional athlete. Although I am no professional athlete, I still dream big every day. This is my dream. It is my dream to share my story, to serve others, to spread the joy. I have created it for myself with a lot of hard work and discipline.

Phew. We finally sat down for a subway ride back to Manhattan. It was a quick one to Wall Street, and here is where the energy dial got turned up. In a sequential snapshot, my night went like this. Keep up with me here. We got off the subway and walked over to the 9/11 Memorial. I went a few nights before, but was unable to access the monuments then. I couldn't believe I was staring heroism in the face. A nation of one people, many courageously risking their lives in honor of their service, to the people in danger, one unexpected day. I was honored to be standing with the individuals whose spirit will live forever, and I could feel it. I paid my respects, as did everyone else who was surrounding the waterfalls. I walked away thinking to myself that life is short. You're here today, gone tomorrow. It can happen just like that. Very quickly. *I better live fully every single day, or I am going to have regrets!*

It was approaching 6:00 p.m. and my two friends decided to head back to the hotel for some rest before the late night fun would start. I was sitting at Park Place Station trying to figure out whether I should go back home, take a nap, and clean up before going out with the rest of the crew.

"No!" I said to myself right there. "I am in New York, full of pulsing energy right now, plus I have some items on my to-do list I could cross off." I was on a tour of the city, and I was going to see as much as I could. I bypassed resting and took the uptown two train to the Fourteenth Street stop where Henry suggested I meet him. He showed me the popular MacDougal and Bleecker Streets. Every corner in New York was full of life. Every time I got off a train and walked up the stairs, outside onto the street level, I was entering a brand new theme park. There were tons of sub cities on the island and each had such distinct qualities. I was constantly surprised with my eyes wide open. I marched through the West Village and got a crash course on the history there while chomping on some famous New York pizza. I topped off my pig hunger with a giant crepe from the Creperie. I had banana and Nutella with whipped cream. The shop was big enough for a cash register and two human bodies. Its storage was directly above the heads of the service staff. A folding ladder was suspended to reach the upper area. I was so impressed. *These folks were doing so much with so little, and finding ways to make people happy.*

After pigging out and stuffing my belly, I continued to walk around in awe. Just then, I caught a glimpse of the Washington Square Arch. It was shining brightly like a diamond in the distance and, like a kid, I said, "Oooooo, let's go there!" Washington Square Park is synonymous with celebrating nonconformity, which I stand by with all of my heart. I have a quote that reads:

"If you want to stand out from the majority, you must be and do differently than the majority. Conformity is the most certain path to mediocrity and the imprisonment of your highest self."

Dare to be one that separates from the ordinary and explores a new pathway.

This park was a landmark and I had had it on my list. Check! It was evening time now, but the park's features were robust. Children were playing, dogs were running around, and, again, tourists like me were taking photos of every detail. I could even smell the beauty in the flowers and in the gardens. Benches were occupied with couples making out, and picnic tables were playing host to a variety of park visitors talking about shopping on the adjacent Fifth Avenue. Ah, Fifth Avenue? Here I was, still going. I was going to take on all of New York this night, and no tranquilizer would be able to neutralize me. Henry left at this point, so the remainder of my night would be on my own and, I was totally fine with that.

I went north on Fifth Avenue, staring up, left and right. Sometimes I was dodging cars, because I was almost making the fatal mistake of not paying attention to red and green lights. The traffic in the city was the truth! I had to watch it. I passed the Flatiron Building, and checked it off my list. I captured more photos. I passed the 40/40 Club, and thought about Jay-Z (HOVA), and his impact on the city. I even stopped to give a homeless man all of the spare dollars bills and change I had in my pocket from the day, because it was cold, he was outside, and I was sure he would make good use of it.

By now I was getting close to Madison Square Garden. I went from visiting one New York basketball arena earlier in the day to the second. I will admit, I was rejoicing at my arrival at The Garden, a venue committed to providing world-class entertainment and sporting events. It's famous for basketball, hockey, concerts, wrestling, ice shows—you name it. I circled the venue, taking as many pictures as allowed without having the security team chase me off the grounds. It was dreamy for me. There were posters from past performers lining the walls and profiles of the current Knicks and Rangers teams. I even got one picture with the Garden and the Empire State Building in the background in the same frame. Guess where I was headed next? Yes, I was about to head up, to stand tall on top of the world! This was my moment, and I was still full of excitement. Off I went a few short blocks over.

When I arrived at the Empire State Building, I was staring up at this gigantic needlelike building. I thought to myself, "Stand a little taller and make each day a little better than the one before." I felt like this was the pinnacle of my trip so far, and for good reason. So where do I start? Well, getting in the damn building is the first thing that comes to mind, Manny, but I was so excited that I went into the wrong entrance, only to have one of the staff usher me to the correct one. I'm inside.

What's next? There were several options for exploration. Do I get a pass to go up eighty-six floors? Or do I get the pass plus the separate pass where I get access the 102nd floor? I said, *"No regrets"* and went with 102! The educational content was mind-boggling. The information about the building's history, and what it took to get it upright, blew my mind. I didn't know I was capable of being so enlightened after such a long day, but the headsets and plaques of information kept me engaged.

When I arrived at floor eighty-six, after dancing with the elevator attendant and taking pictures, I almost lost my breath. It was considerably windy, but the sense of freedom I found on top of the building was that of a man who had found his soul and his reason for living. I circled the observation deck countless times. I felt like each time I circled I was seeing something new. My mind was in the clouds, this time not because I was almost dead, but because I was living my life on my terms. I could see miles in every direction. To the south was One World Trade Center, standing tall with us; to the north, I could see the bright lights of Times Square and the dark shadow of Central Park just off in the distance. To the east, I could see the Chrysler Building and the Queens borough of New York. To the west, I could see the Hudson River and New Jersey in the distance. How did I get so lucky to be so fortunate to explore all of life's greatest people, places, and things? I felt like I was flying. There is no greater feeling in the world than when you are in complete control, making this happen for yourself. And you bet your life, I had earned the feeling!

Oh my gosh! I could write an entire book about this trip alone, but I wanted to get the meat and potatoes in writing here. Now, I want to bring your attention to Tuesday, January 19, three days later. This particular Tuesday morning was much different from what I just described, a lot more physically relaxing, but just as fulfilling and more rewarding, as I came to an interesting conclusion. I woke up in a stranger's apartment at ninety-five Wall Street, the same one I had booked on Airbnb. After I woke up, changed clothes, and went upstairs, I chose to get in a nice morning run and workout in the building's gym. It was my new morning routine, to get some sort of exercise in just after waking. By the time I had worked up a sweat and checked the time, I had to get ready for a 10:45 a.m. stranger meet-up in the upper west side, at Magnolia Bakery on Columbus and Sixty-Ninth Street.

Any guesses about whom I was meeting there? I hopped on the uptown two train. By this time, I was becoming an expert at understanding the subway system. I only had to ride one line the whole time, so that made it easy. I got off at the Seventy-Second Street exit, walked one block east and three blocks south to the bakery. I was meeting Karen, the lady from Brooklyn I had met days before. She was kind enough to make time for me in between her appointments.

We had a fabulous yet simple hour together. She looked like my mother did. I was right where I was supposed to be at every step of the way. She opened me up to a developing side of me, she had a great story, and I am so happy that I met this woman! On our exit, she reached out to me and said, "Here, I wanted you to have this." It was a quarter-sized custom button. On one side was the cheetah; on the reverse side it read *inner guidance*. "This is your reference point," she said, smiling. I still have it sitting right next to me, guiding me along, as I write this.

I walked away with the conviction that my path was unfolding right in front of me. My spirit was flourishing. I was manifesting my greatest desires. And it came from the decision to stop drinking. I continued to walk south, back toward Central Park. I stopped at the Time Warner Center and stood up against the ledge, looking out the window and into south Central Park. I was light as a feather; my life was fully existing in its spiritual form.

The rest of my day included lunch on my own at Brooklyn Diner, a few blocks above Times Square. I enjoyed the peace and didn't need any company. It was a pleasant idea, and I listened and watched the people next to me talk about work, relationships, and money. I smiled and just loved them, agape, that's all. After I paid my bill and walked outside, I was greeted by Broadway Street. I split the heart of Times Square with my head on a swivel, fascinated with the allure of the tall buildings lining the block. It was all personality, and

I was certainly enamored just before I boarded the two train south to head home. I had a fancy dinner in just a few hours back west, in Chelsea. After dinner, I finished the long day with a short stroll around town and a nice full-body massage in the financial district. It was certainly the right choice on my part, as I was practicing extreme self-care and love. I was my top priority now.

The beautiful part of this weeklong trip? This day, January 19, was my thirtieth birthday. I had found a way to find joy in the absence of what used to make me happy—partying, drinking, drugs, desperate need for companionship, or someone to give me something so I could feel like I was worth something. On this day, I didn't feel like I turned thirty. I felt like I was born again! Only now I was wiser, united with my purpose and in complete control of my life. I wasn't looking for outside circumstances to support my peace anymore. It was an inside job, a job I was working hard at every day. I realized that the most important things in life aren't things and, because I had raised the standards for my life and created a path for the life I wanted to live, I was staying consistent with who I now defined myself as—spontaneous, fulfilled, joyful. I am fulfilled, because I chose to see the light despite all of the dark. Stay positive my friends, you are all amazing, gifted, and worth more than you know. Express your best self! Someone needs you, today, right now. There are many stories and countless social and cultural expectations about "how you should live your life," but I say don't listen to them. Take time for yourself and create the life you have always wanted. Live your life to the fullest every single day! There is no better time than now to live your life on your terms!

You are living!

You are loving!

You are learning!

And now, the choice is yours…